BLACKIE THE BRUMBY

This edition published 2018
By Living Book Press
Copyright © The Estate of C.K. Thompson, 1951

The publisher would like to give a huge 'Thank You' to the author's family
for their assistance in making this book available once more.

ISBN: 978-1-925729-00-9

A catalogue record for this
book is available from the
National Library of Australia

BLACKIE THE BRUMBY

By C.K. Thompson

King of the Ranges
Old Bob's Birds
Maggie the Magnificent
Thunderbolt the Falcon
Monarch of the Western Skies
Wild Canary
Warrigal the Warrior
Blackie the Brumbie
Willy Wagtail
Red Emperor
Tiger Cat
Wombat

CONTENTS

FOREWORD

For many years, wild horses in Australia have been known as "brumbies," but how the name originated is a mystery that I have been unable to solve.

Dictionaries and standard works of reference all agree that the origin of the name is obscure. Pioneers, bushmen, men who have lived in the Outback all their lives, hold different views and are ready to back their opinions to the point of fist fights.

One authority ventures the suggestion that the name possibly has been derived from a Queensland aboriginal word which sounds like "*booramby*" or "*buroomby*", meaning "wild" or "untamed."

There is a theory that the title comes from the surname of a man named William Brumby, who was said to be a famous horse-breeder in Queensland many years ago.

Demonstrating the wide diversion of opinion, however, is the legend that has currency in the Monaro district of New South Wales, that a horse-breeding family named Brumby, who had a station near Omeo in the early days, has the honour.

As the legend was told to me, the Brumby family was a little careless with its horses, allowing many to run wild in the bush. Other station-owners, and stockmen, noticing these straying around, would say... "Those horses are Brumby's."

During my long search for the truth, a rather novel suggestion was put to me—that the brumby got his name from "*Brummagem*." This used to be a contemptuous title for the great English manufacturing city of Birmingham and meant "cheap and showy" or not the real thing. It alluded to the counterfeit money that was made there in the 17th century—coins that were sometimes called "brummies." I do not place any reliance in the "Brummagem" definition for, after all, the brumby cannot be regarded as "not the real thing." He is a real horse, even if he is a wild one.

I must, in passing, make special reference to the chapter in this book, "School Interlude." Though not, perhaps, chronologically accurate as regards the verse quoted, that episode, in itself, is based on fact. Something very like it happened in my own school days.

I went to a bush school with a lad we knew as "Jonah" and in "School Interlude" and subsequent chapters, I have painted an accurate picture of him as a boy. "Jonah" and I were great mates and had many humourous and exciting adventures together. Some day I hope to write a book about "Jonah" who was, and still is today, what is known colloqui-ally as "a hard citizen."

One of my first horse rides was on an animal secured for me by "Jonah" without his father's permission. During an exhilarating gallop I was thrown off, and as I lay half-stunned on the ground, I heard, faintly, the voice of "Jonah" roaring, "Hey, what are you laying down there for? Get up and catch that dashed horse. My old man will belt the daylights out of me if anything happens to it and I'll belt the daylights out of you if you don't look after it better."

That was "Jonah." It didn't matter if my neck was broken as long as his father's precious horse was uninjured.

But they were good old days, boys and girls. I hope that you, in your own way, have enjoyed many happy adventures and will enjoy many more.

And may I be permitted to hope, too, that you will enjoy many happy hours reading *"Blackie the Brumby."*

-C. K. THOMPSON.

DEDICATION

To my good friend and fellow
Honorary Magistrate,
CEC. BORHAM, J.P.,
of Hamilton, N.S.W.,
who knows and loves horses.

CHAPTER I

THE STOLEN THOROUGHBRED

IT had been a hot and breathless day—one of those so typical of an Australian mid-summer when even the most hardened of the bush creatures find life tedious.

Dusk, however, had brought with it a faint breeze which, stirring the tired leaves of the stately gums, gave promise of a mild night.

The first stars were diamond-studding the velvet of the heavens as a little cavalcade of horses, their unshod hoofs rattling not unmusically upon loose stones, made its way down out of the hills, first to water at the nearest pool, then to graze.

There were fifteen horses in the band, led by a large black stallion. Blacks, bays and roans, they followed him obediently and confidently, knowing that at the first hint of danger, he would be ready to defend them against all comers.

These were no ordinary horses, but wild, untamed brumbies, as much denizens of the Australian bush as the kangaroos, emus and 'possums. They were not, of course, truly native Australians, their ancestors having been imported from other lands across the seas, but not one of them had ever experienced the subduing influence of the hand of man.

In the great Outback, fences were practically unknown. Station owners allowed their horses to roam almost at will; and many horses that had found their way into the mountains and out on to the plains, preferred the free life there to the working round, and had remained.

And so they lived and bred and, in many cases, became pests—breaking into cultivated paddocks and doing more damage in one night than a settler could repair in months. They also lured other horses away from their owners to join them.

The band of fifteen, led by Bushranger, the black stallion, had been in the ranges for some time. They had been driven there by stockmen and others who had made unsuccessful efforts to capture, yard, tame and brand them for useful work. The leader had been named "Bushranger" by a disgusted Stockman who had spent almost a whole day trying to run him to earth. But Bushranger had been one too many for the stockman and had led him on a merry dance before taking to the hilly country where the rest of his scattered band had joined him.

Bushranger's brumbies regarded the whole of the countryside as their own special domain and they ranged over it at will. They travelled as the fancy took them, and their knowledge of the bush, the mountains and the plains was extensive. Hundreds upon hundreds of miles passed under their restless hoofs, circumstances dictating speed and distance.

Grass and water, of course, were their major bodily needs and when the seasons were good they lazed along as they felt inclined. It often chanced that they would spend several weeks in one locality just loafing around and doing nothing in particular. Again, it often happened that within 24 hours they would be many long miles from their last feeding-ground—and man was generally to blame.

It was nothing new for Bushranger and his band to be hunted by human beings. Sometimes there were organised expeditions against them, and though one or two unfortunates had been separated from the band and captured, Bushranger always escaped.

The brumby band sometimes numbered as many as fifty. There were many wild bush horses and several mobs wandered about as organised communities. It had not been unknown for the membership of these bands to be interchanged; but Bushranger and his select fifteen stuck together.

It was not often that human beings went out deliberately to hunt the brumbies, though that had occurred. It was when the untamed horses ventured close to properties and made havoc among crops that frantic efforts were made either to capture them or to wipe them out.

Bushranger lived up to his name. In addition to being a horse of rare intelligence and a first class fighter, human settlements fascinated him. No matter how long he might remain in the unsettled country of the far Outback, eventually he led his band back to human habitation. He was never so happy as when he was causing a lot of annoyance to settlers by raiding their crops, but he attained the supreme height of delight when he succeeded in luring a horse or mare away from a settlement to join his outlaws.

Naturally this did not make him at all popular with the settlers and it was the understood thing that the man who captured and tamed Bushranger, or shot him dead, would earn the grateful thanks of everybody,

Of all the indignant squatters, the man most upset by Bushranger's depredations was Sir. John Sylvester, whose station property covered thousands of acres, and who numbered among his many horses quite a few well-bred blood stock.

Old Sylvester loved every horse he owned, from the rough and hardy stock animals to the stately thoroughbreds. Among his special favourites had been a mare named Margaret and the old station owner had thought that Margaret was as devoted to him as he was to her. But femininity is ever fickle. Margaret preferred the wild life of the open bush in the company of Bushranger the brumby, to the soft and easy existence of a coddled thoroughbred in a sheltered stable and fenced paddock.

One warm moonlight night in late spring, Bushranger and his band descended from their mountain fastness, kicked down the fence surrounding the paddock that protected Margaret and several other horses, and invited them all to come and have a look at the mountain scenery by moonlight. Margaret and a young colt accepted the invitation, but the others remained where they were.

Neither Sylvester nor his station hands saw Margaret or the colt again. The mare was quite content to range the plains and the bush as the mate of the enterprising Bushranger.

Of course the squatter was wild with rage when he learned what had happened. He did not need the advice of his aboriginal stockman that the wild horses had taken Margaret away. The broken fence and the tell-tale hoof marks all around the place were enough for his own practised eye.

Bushranger, being the intelligent animal he was, did not linger around the place after the theft of the mare. Sylvester had known of the band's haunts in the hills and immediately he found his mare gone, had personally led the rescue party; but none of them caught even a fleeting glimpse of a brumby. The whole band after the raid, the triumphant Bushranger at their head and Margaret just behind him, had made straight for the plains, travelling far and fast. It was hopeless to chase them, so Sylvester gave it up, returning to his station homestead in a far from pleasant mood.

Though the loss of the valuable mare was serious, the matter had its compensations—that part of the country where Sylvester lived became free of brumby depredations. The wild horses had gone—for good, he hoped.

As the weeks passed, the loss of the erring Margaret gradually faded from the minds of the stockmen and station hands, but two people could not forget—old Mr. Sylvester himself, and his young son, George.

George Sylvester, aged eleven, was a sturdy, curly-headed bush-bred boy, who had been brought up on the station with an intense love of horses. To him they were just perfect. Like his father he adored them all, from the shaggiest old stock horse to the noblest of the thoroughbreds. George, however, differed from his father in one respect. He had a good word to say for brumbies while the station owner hated them all.

The lad had lost his mother when he was a small child. What he had learned about horses had been imparted to him by everyone around the place—his father, the stockmen, the boundary riders and last, but by no means least, Black Herbie, the aboriginal horsebreaker and stockboy. What Herbie did not know about horses was not worth learning.

"What do you think of the brumbies now, George?" his father asked him after the disappearance of Margaret. "Do you still think they are fine animals and as good as any of my blood stock?"

"I've never said that, Dad," protested the boy, "but just because they have lived in the bush instead of in stables and paddocks does not mean that they are no good at all."

"They are perfect pests," said his father. "As for comparing them with station horses, why, they have no breed at all. They are any and all sorts. Of course they are tough and hardy. They would have to be or they would never survive their rough life.

"But I'm getting away from the subject. I asked you what you thought of the brumbies now that they have stolen Margaret."

Young George looked thoughtful. He did love all sorts of horses. Yet he did feel keenly the loss of the mare. Still, he wanted to be fair if he could.

"Of course, Dad," he said, "we mustn't altogether blame the brumbies. What about Margaret herself? She didn't have to go, did she? I don't suppose old Bushranger bailed her up with a gun and forced her to run away."

"Oh, I have no doubt she went willingly enough," grunted the squatter. "That isn't the point. If these brumby villains were all destroyed, as they should be, no horse owner would have to put up with these losses."

He became, suddenly, most indignant.

"Just you think of it," he exclaimed. "Just you think of that lovely, well-bred mare out there somewhere in the bush being knocked about and injured by wild and rough horses."

"Don't say that, Dad," begged the boy.

"She won't last a week," his father went on. "How in the name of fortune will she be able to stand up to that life? Why, she has never been handled or treated other than with kindness since she was a little foal."

Tears began to gather in young George's eyes as he considered the picture painted by his father. Margaret undoubtedly would miss the easy life of the Sylvester station.

"Perhaps she will come back to us, Dad," said George hopefully.

"Not her!" snorted his father. "Do you think Bushranger and his gang of thugs will let her? They'd kick her to death first. She's miles away now, probably lying in some rocky gully with her legs broken."

"Oh, don't talk like that, Dad!" cried young George in anguish. "I can't bear to think of anything like that happening to Margaret."

He broke off and gulped, hard. "I hate the brumbies now. I'd like to kill them all," he said.

"That's the boy," applauded the old man. "Keep on thinking like that and we'll make something of you yet. Of course they should all be destroyed. Ah, well, you go on with your reading. I have to look at a few things around the homestead."

After his father had left the room, young George picked up his book, but he could not concentrate on the printed pages.

His thoughts were hundreds of miles away with the brumby herd and Margaret. What his father had said about the possibility of Margaret being harmed, had effected him deeply. For a while he toyed with the idea of packing a camping bag, saddling his own private horse, Ginger, and setting out in search of the missing mare. He would camp on the track until he found her, no matter how long it took or how hard the way might be.

As the idea took shape in his mind, he pushed his book aside and gave himself up wholly to thinking it out. What a triumph it would he if he could locate the band, lure Margaret away from it and return with her to his father! What a proud moment that would be! The boy's eyes glistened at the very thought of it.

But Margaret had been gone now for more than a week. All the experienced stockmen sent out by his father had failed to catch up with the band. Black Herbie, noted tracker and horseman that he was, might have succeeded, but he had been away mending fences in one of the further-out runs at the time. He had only just returned and when asked by Mr. Sylvester what he thought of the chances of recapturing the mare, had replied that since there had been rain over portion of the territory and since the band probably had scattered far and wide, the chances of catching up with it were very slim.

As young George turned this over in his mind, he came to the reluctant conclusion that where Black Herbie would fail, he himself had no chance of success. George was a sensible boy and though prone to day-dreaming like any other normal lad of his age, he realised his own limitations.

With a sigh, he dismissed horses from his mind, at least temporarily, and, giving up all thoughts of trying to read a book, left the house and wandered down to the harness shed where he devoted half an hour to polishing his saddle and bridle, which were already clean.

It was holiday time. George attended a small bush school with about twenty other children from the township and neighbouring stations, riding there each day on his horse, Ginger. He had no special boy friends because they all lived long distances from his home. His special friends were the station horses.

CHAPTER II.
THE COMING OF BLACKIE

BUSHRANGER and his mob ranged far and wide as the weeks and months passed. They did not stay in any one locality for very long. Years of experience had taught the intelligent stallion that raids on human property were always followed by reprisals on the part of those raided. When mares were lured away from properties, the reprisals were heavier.

In his time, Bushranger had raided many places. Sometimes necessity drove him to do so. In seasons of drought when grass and water were scarce on the plains he loved, he often raided settled areas to obtain food. Occasionally he swooped down upon a human habitation from sheer high spirits, damaging fences and other property for no reason at all.

But his greatest pleasure lay in tempting mares away from their human owners. He had done it so often and escaped unscathed that he had a supreme contempt for men and all their works. His inborn sense of caution, however, never led him to make mistakes. If familiarity with humans bred a certain contempt, it did not make him careless.

Though Bushranger himself had always escaped unharmed when hunted after raids, members of his band had, from time to time, paid the penalty. Many had been shot by pursuing white men, others had been rounded up and led back to the despoiled property, there to become common beasts of burden. It was common justice that there should be replacements of stolen horses, but the big stallion did not think of that. Actually, he thought of nothing but himself, though he did look after the welfare of his band in times of danger.

Bushranger, at this stage, led a mob of sixteen, including Margaret. It would not remain at that strength forever. The time would come when the young colts would be kicked out to make their own ways in the world, found their own mobs, or lead the lives of hermits.

Apart from the stallion himself, there were nine mares, one of which was Margaret, four fillies and two well grown colts. The colts in time would grow into mature stallions, but before they reached that stage, Bushranger would hunt them from the mob.

He wanted no rivals. It was the way of the wild—one stallion was always the leader, generally of just a little band of mares. Colts that grew into stallions were a menace to leadership and the wise chief gave them hidings and hunted them away before they had the strength to challenge his kingship.

Bushranger, of course, knew all about this without having to be told. Back of his brain was the knowledge that in the fullness of time when old age dimmed his physical and mental powers, there would arise a hardy youngster who would refuse to be driven away. That youngster would fight him and conquer him and that would be the end of Bushranger. He might be left to die, or he might escape with his life, to roam the country alone.

It was in this manner that Bushranger himself had gained the leadership of a band. He had fought and conquered the old stallion that had been the leader and, after having beaten him to the ground with two broken legs, had left him there to die while he himself had galloped off in triumph with the deposed leader's harem.

Bushranger, with Margaret at his side, and the rest of the mob trailing close behind arrived, after many weeks of travelling, at open country which was very familiar to him. It was many long miles from the nearest human settlement and the wild horses shared it only with wandering bands of kangaroos.

Far to the east and just visible in the sun-drenched haze, rose the mountain range in the gloom heights of which was the source of a gay little babbling brook that, winding downwards, turned into a large creek and finally, becoming a river, made its way across the plains like a giant brown snake.

With water and grass in plenty, long stretches of flat country over which they could stretch their legs in exhilarating gallops, the brumbies settled down for a long stay.

Bushranger had often been here. If it could ever be said that he possessed a home, this was it. Invariably he retired here after some daring raid on a human property. It was his holiday resort where he came to rest and relax.

And it was here, where years earlier, Bushranger himself had been born, that Blackie first saw the light of an Australian day.

Bushranger was not very interested in the birth of his son. The old veteran, in his long and exciting life, had seen many such youngsters arrive in the world and subsequently take their places in the wild horse community. They meant nothing to him and neither did Blackie. He felt no pride in the spindly-legged, awkward colt trotting at the side of his mother.

It would not be true, however, to say that Bushranger completely disregarded the new arrival. A horse of wide experience, had it been left to him to direct the ways of the equine world, he would have placed a ban on the birth of all foals, colt or filly. When they were young they were nuisances, hampering the movements of the band, which could not travel as fast as Bushranger wanted when certain circumstances demanded it.

If the black stallion was more or less indifferent to Blackie from a fatherly point of view, Margaret definitely was not. The colt might be awkward and unattractive; but he was her son—her first foal—and he was her major care. In fact, he occupied most of her spare time.

Blackie resembled his mother in that he had a similar white blaze on his forehead and a white stocking on his left hind leg. Old Bushranger was completely black.

The brumby band was in no hurry to leave that country, at least Bushranger was not, and that meant the whole band, of course. They did not, however, hang around in any one spot. The plains were vast and the band was wild and free. The horses grazed about where the fancy of Bushranger took them. Sometimes they would linger in one vicinity for a couple of days, then Bushranger, acting on impulse and feeling like a frisky young colt, would suddenly throw his heels into the air, snort defiantly at nothing in particular, and gallop madly into the distance, covering perhaps five miles before dropping into a canter, then a trot, finally to slow down to an idle grazing walk. On these occasions, those who could keep up with him, did; those who couldn't, toiled in the rear, but eventually rejoined the main band.

In brumby fashion, the personnel of the band changed slightly from time to time as some members felt the urge to move on, and odd strays joined up. Bushranger always regarded any newcomers with suspicion. Any lusty young colts that might eventually challenge his leadership, were firmly ordered to move on. If they objected, they were assisted on their way by a none too gentle application of a pair of iron-hard hoofs or two sets of perfectly vicious teeth.

Blackie grew fast and it was not long before he felt independent of his mother as a source of nourishment and protection. There were no other youngsters of his age in the band. The juvenile members were fast nearing the stage when they would regard themselves as grown-up horses.

There was one young colt, a handsome chestnut, who rather fancied himself as the leader of the mob. He was not afraid of Bushranger, yet he did not mean to try conclusions with that old warrior until he was completely sure of his chances.

Bushranger, self-sufficient and self-reliant animal though he was, was not unaware of this. The big black stallion knew that this young chestnut was the only horse likely to contest his right to lead the band. For one thing, he was the biggest and strongest of the colts. The original mob had consisted of nine mares, two colts and four fillies and, of course, the mighty Bushranger himself. Then Blackie had come along. Two of the fillies had left the band, but they had been replaced by three stray colts.

Yes, Bushranger considered, of the five young males in his following, the chestnut, Red Eagle, was the logical aspirant for the leadership title.

Early one morning, just after the band had watered at a creek, Bushranger decided to take action. He was a horse who believed in getting in first when trouble was brewing, or likely to brew.

Up to this moment, Red Eagle had only been playing with the idea of challenging the black stallion. He had been turning the idea over in his mind, and liking it very much. But he was not quite ready for action.

Bushranger led his brumbies from the creek to high flat ground and when they began grazing, he quietly drew away from them. He grazed slowly for perhaps two hundred yards and then, without the slightest warning, swung round, gave a loud, piercing scream, and dashed straight at Red Eagle. Rearing up on his hind legs, he brought his front hoofs dashing down upon the unprepared colt's back. Before that startled horse could recover from the shock, the black stallion slewed round, put down his head, snorted, and let Red Eagle have both his hind hoofs clean in the ribs.

Red Eagle was an intelligent animal that could accept a hit. He saw that he wasn't wanted in those parts, and when Bushranger dashed at him and bit a mouthful of flesh out of his shoulder, he gave up all thoughts and hopes of brumby leadership, and proceeded to place as many miles as possible between himself and the black terror.

Bushranger watched him careening across the plains for a few moments and then, with a snort of contempt, threw a sweeping glance over the rest of the band as if to ask if any member thereof desired to start something. None did, so the stallion resumed his grazing.

As the weeks and months passed, Bushranger moved slowly westwards, the band, of course, trailing along with him. The country to which he led them was most unattractive because it was on the fringe of the desert. Why Bushranger should decide to visit this land, only he himself knew, because there was nothing of interest there, not even good grazing; while of creeks and natural water there were hardly any.

They were still poking around here when summer came on them. The hot sun soon parched the grass and the pickings they got from desert trees and bushes were not enough to keep the band in good condition. The sole watering place now was a hole in the bed of a creek that was fast evaporating and before summer was well advanced, it had dried up completely, forcing the brumbies to dig for water, which they did—using their forefeet most efficiently.

What perverse trait in his nature kept Bushranger in that

unattractive desert land is hard to determine, but stay there he did, much to the disgust of the rest of the band, particularly Margaret, the station-bred mare. She was not born to this kind of life, and though she was still devoted to Bushranger, she was fast getting fed up with everything. It was all right when they were in good country, but this was the limit, and she yearned for the comfort, ease and regular meals at the Sylvester station.

As the days grew hotter and hotter and as Bushranger still persisted in hanging around the desert, Margaret reached a decision. She was going home. It was easy for her to reach such a decision, but not so easy for her to carry it out. She did not know where her old home was. The horses had travelled hundreds of miles over all sorts of country in the two years she had been a member of the brumby band.

Blackie, who by this time was a well grown animal, had no personal thoughts about the matter of neighbourhood. He went where the mob went. It was the only life he knew. He had never laid eyes on a human being in the whole of his short existence.

There came a hot, breathless night when the brumbies were bedded down under a group of scraggy trees on the bank of the dry creek. Margaret, who had been brooding over things all day, reached a firm resolve—she was leaving right now.

She got to her feet and shook herself vigorously. Then she looked at the rest of the band stretched out on the hard earth, some asleep, others just resting, more or less comfortably.

Bushranger, seeing Margaret on her feet, also stood up. So did Blackie. Bushranger advanced with mincing steps and rubbed his nose against Margaret's neck. The mare laid back her ears and bared her teeth at him. Bushranger looked surprised, but knowing the ways of women—creatures who never knew what they wanted—repeated the caress. Margaret resented it by giving a shrill neigh and pig-rooting with her front feet. She bared her teeth again and made a vicious snap at her lord and master. Bushranger was taken aback and ceased his caresses.

Margaret eyed him thoughtfully for a moment or two and then, turning her back on him, trotted away into the darkness. Bushranger threw back his head, yawned mightily and then indolently dropped to the ground. He rolled over, stretched out his legs, gave a loud sigh, and lay still. His whole attitude was that of a long-suffering husband philosophically putting up with his wife's nagging tantrums.

Blackie looked in the direction where his mother had vanished, wondering where she had gone. Perhaps she knew where there was grass and water. If so, he wanted to share it with her.

The youngster caught up with his mother before she had gone very far. Margaret was trotting steadily forward, looking neither to the right nor to the left. She was going home and she felt in her heart that her homing instinct would get her there. She did not heed Blackie's arrival, though she knew it was he who was trotting just behind her. If he wanted to come along, well and good. If not, let him stay with Bushranger. She was not interested in Blackie and his whims. If he still wanted to be mothered by her, she thought, as she trotted along, then he was out of luck.

The country here was arid and stony, but that did not worry the two horses. Margaret had long since grown used to it and Blackie had been born to it.

They had travelled, perhaps, three miles, the mare in front and her strapping son a few yards in the rear, when the sound of galloping hoofs behind them made them both prick up their ears, but did not halt them. Closer and closer and louder and louder came the wild tattoo of hard hoofs on hard ground, until presently it sounded at their side and then, as a dark form flashed by, in front of them.

It was Bushranger. The big black stallion wheeled to a halt about a dozen yards ahead and faced the mare and colt, savage indignation glinting in his fiery eyes. Margaret and Blackie halted, the colt ranging at the side of his mother, and they both stared at the big black stallion.

A whistling kind of neigh rent the air, strong and menacing, as Bushranger voiced his protests. Who did they think they were, running out on him like this? Who was boss around here, anyway?

He marched up to Margaret and, with a quick movement, shoved his nose under her mouth and suddenly jerked his head upwards, sending Margaret's high in the air. It was a reproof that Margaret resented. She whinnied, laid back her ears and made a vicious snap at him. He backed slightly and bumped into Blackie who, growing excited, stretched out his head and nipped his father smartly on the neck.

Bushranger, snorting with indignation that this whipper-snapper son of his should have the temerity to attack him, swung round and shot out both heels, Blackie receiving them on the shoulder. It was not a hard blow, but it was a plain direction from Bushranger for his son to keep his nose out of this argument and mind his own business before he got hurt.

Blackie retired a few paces and brooded a bit. Margaret began to trot forward again, but Bushranger ran in front of her and turned her back. Squealing her rage, the mare swung round and set off at a canter the way she and Blackie had come, but after she had gone a short distance, she began to circle, intending to get around the big black stallion and continue her homeward journey. Bushranger, however, was up to that old trick. Taking a short cut, he headed her off again and Margaret stopped dead as if in doubt what to do next.

Then Bushranger changed his tactics. Wheeling about her, whinnying softly, he arched his magnificent neck and gently rubbed his head against her. She snorted and whirled away from him, but he followed and repeated the performance. Soon he had her headed in the direction he wanted her to go—back to the band—and with soothing whistles and affectionate caresses, got her to see it his way.

Blackie, still brooding, was undecided whether to follow them or to stay where he was. He pondered the matter for a minute or two and then arrived at the conclusion that it would be nicer back with the band than wandering alone in the desert without a friend.

Setting off at a fast trot, he caught up with his parents who were now travelling amicably, side by side. Margaret had changed her mind about going home.

When Blackie ranged up alongside Bushranger, he got a rude shock. The stallion gave a loud scream of hate which told Blackie quite plainly that he wasn't wanted. The colt did not believe that his father meant it, and continued to trot at his side.

What an infernal nuisance this youngster was! Couldn't he take a broad hint? Bushranger, without wasting breath in idle whinnying or neighing, rolled his eyes and seized a goodly portion of Blackie's mane in his large and vicious teeth. The sharp tug he gave made Blackie scream with pain. But when Bushranger let the mane go and bit his son hard on the neck, the youngster screamed louder.

Blackie was quite taken aback by this attack, and hurt, too. His father, however, gave him no time for self-pity. The stallion was annoyed and showed it. Rearing up on his hind legs he brought his forefeet down sharply, the iron-hard hoofs raking two long tears in Blackie's hide from the neck to the belly. Blackie whistled his agony and gave a full-throated scream when he felt his father's hind hoofs rattling against his ribs.

That was more than sufficient. Bushranger had at last convinced his thick-headed son that as far as the brumby herd was concerned, he was through, washed-up and finished. Like the hard-hearted father in a sad melodrama telling his erring son to be gone and never darken the family doorway again, Bushranger threw Blackie a last, withering, warning look before he whirled away to rejoin Margaret who had watched the scene a short distance away. Then they galloped off together.

Blackie watched them until they had vanished into the star-studded desert night, and then he turned away disconsolately, a horse without a single friend.

Daylight found him wandering aimlessly along. He picked gloomily at sparse tufts of tasteless grass and sadly flicked his tail at the swarms of flies which insisted on investigating his wounds. The hot sun eventually forced him to seek shade and this he found at the side of a huge pile of rocks sprawled in the middle of the sandy waste. There was neither water nor grass here, but there was shade, and the young brumby collapsed in the lee of a big rock, first to roll in the dust and then to lie still, fretting over his wounds and his personal troubles. The latter, in fact, troubled him more than the former, which were not at all serious.

He lingered in the shade for several hours, but thirst finally made him move. He had to find water somewhere. The sun troubled him as did the swarms of flies which seemed to materialise out of the hot air.

He had not the slightest idea what he was going to do, but he wandered along, hour after hour, until late afternoon when something in a slight breeze that had sprung up made him pause, his head high in the air. He knew that delicious smell! There was water not far away!

Heading straight in the direction from which the breeze was blowing, the brumby sighted a small clump of trees far to the right. He immediately shot off at a tangent, heading for those trees, and when he reached them, found that they grew on the edge of a small waterhole. There was not much water in it, but it was enough for Blackie. He gulped down almost as much sand, mud and clay as he did water, but that did not trouble him. He had sampled much worse.

There was a little grass near the hole and Blackie decided to stay there for a time. As night fell, the waterhole was visited by kangaroos, wallabies and other smaller animals, while a flock of noisy cockatoos roosted in the trees overhead. None of these took much notice of the brumby.

Blackie left the waterhole late in the afternoon of the fourth day, making directly eastwards. Instinct told him that there was better grass not far away, and instinct did not let him down.

He trotted through a belt of stunted trees and then came to a halt. About a quarter of a mile away was a large tract of grassy land and, grazing peacefully thereon, was a small mob of horses!

The brumby had had no idea that representatives of his kind were so close. The waterhole he had left could not be more than ten miles away. The fact that these horses had not visited it showed that there was water nearer.

Indecision made Blackie stay glued to the one spot for quite three minutes. He did not know if this was his old band. If it was and Bushranger were there, Blackie intended to depart elsewhere. At last he began to walk slowly forwards, all his senses on the alert.

Far away in the distance he could see the faint blue outline of a mountain range, apparently well timbered. Closer at hand was flat country, well grassed.

As Blackie neared the little mob of horses, he paused and took close stock of them. There were seven altogether, all seemingly mature animals. He could see no youngsters. At the distance he was he could not distinguish the leader. All the horses were grazing and apparently unaware of his presence.

Blackie had quite recovered from the rough handling he had received at the teeth and hoofs of his father and yearned for the companionship of his kind. He was no hermit.

When he got closer, he observed, with pleasure, that Bushranger was not among those present. Neither was Margaret. That was good.

Standing with his head high in the air and watching the band closely, he was suddenly startled to hear behind him a loud whinny. Slewing round he saw a big flea-bitten grey stallion only a few yards away. Where on earth had he come from?

What Blackie did not know was that this grey was the leader of the little band. He had been away on business of his own that afternoon, business connected with certain horses in a distant station paddock which he intended to lure away to join his band. He was returning when he sighted this lone stranger and had caught up with him without disclosing his presence.

The grey resented the intrusion and intended to demonstrate the fact. He saw before him a powerful young horse which might be a dangerous handful, but he intended to vanquish him. Blackie, silently taking the newcomer's measure, saw before him a handsome, well-formed horse with inquisitive eyes widened, nostrils dilated and splendid neck arched. And yet Blackie was not in the least afraid. No son of the mighty Bushranger had ever been a coward.

Uttering loud and challenging snorts, the grey stallion wheeled round and galloped away, presently turning and running a complete circle around Blackie, who, remembering his father's attack on him, pivoted slowly to keep an eye on it. The grey, continuing to circle, but gradually spiralling nearer, was a grand sight, its mane flying and its tail streaming behind it.

Stopping suddenly, the grey threw his heels high in the air and gave a short exhibition of buckjumping. Blackie watched him silently. Having shown off his might in this fashion, the grey gave a loud snort and came at Blackie with a vicious rush. Getting close, he reared up, but when he brought his forefeet crashing down, Blackie wasn't there. The grey gathered himself for another plunge, but before he could do so, Blackie dashed in and bit him on the neck.

That started it. Within seconds they were at each other, teeth bared, biting and striking with front feet and lashing with their heels.

Squealing loudly and neighing defiantly, the two horses ran side by side, snapping and striking at each other as they did so. Blood was trickling from the wounds on each body, but they cared nothing for that. Soon each was in a lather of sweat, while foam flew from their jaws. Once Blackie got in a very heavy blow on the grey's chest, knocking him down on his tail. The grey sat there thoughtfully for a few seconds like a tired dog, before bounding to his feet. The propulsion sent him straight at Blackie and he sank his teeth into the black's shoulder. It was painful and Blackie screamed savagely. This seemed to infuriate the grey, for it tried to strike him with its front hoofs while savaging him with its teeth.

Wrenching himself free, blood running from his wound, Blackie swung round and let the grey have it with both hind feet. The blow was a terrific one. It caught the grey on the side, knocking it completely off its feet.

And as it lay there in the dust unable to rise, Blackie calmly brought his front feet down on its prostrate body again and again. The black horse was now completely submerged with the fighting blood lust. The son of Bushranger continued to pound the unfortunate grey until life left it.

Satisfied that his rival was dead, Blackie gave a loud and triumphant neigh and galloped off, without invitation, to join the small band that had watched the fight from a distance. He was received without demonstration. Blackie ran his eye over the band. Seven mares. No young and hefty colts or stallions to challenge him. He was glad of that. His wounds were not serious, but he did not relish the prospect of a second fight so soon after the first.

Feeling pleased with himself, Blackie dropped into the usual brumby routine and his harem was quite content to string along with him.

CHAPTER III.

THE CAPTURE OF BLACKIE

THE two stockmen, Harry Hornsby and Norman Preston, had been in the saddle since early morning, riding the out-back paddocks and foothills searching for stray cattle and horses. It had been a long and lazy ride with not much in the way of work, and at noon they rested in the shade of a clump of bushes on the bank of a small creek in a gully walled in by high cliffs.

Neither man had troubled to tie up his horse, merely allowing the reins to dangle, satisfied that the animals would not wander off.

It was while he was eating that Preston's attention was drawn to the unusual behaviour of his mare, Judy. The stockhorse, a sturdy animal, had been quietly grazing, but suddenly she raised her head and whinnied. Preston looked round, but could see nothing unusual. Then he noticed that the mare's gaze was directed upwards as if something on top of the cliffs interested her.

Twisting round and glancing in the same direction, Preston saw something that brought him to his feet with an exclamation.

"What's up, Norm?" asked his mate.

"Stone the crows, Harry, do you see what I see?" cried Preston.

Following his gaze, Hornsby saw, on a large bare rock at the top of the cliffs, a magnificent black stallion sharp-etched

28

against the blue sky. As dark as midnight, the stallion stood there, wild and proud, directing a haughty stare at the men and their horses below.

And as they stared back in astonishment and admiration, Blackie, for it was he, gave a shrill whistle, which echoed among the rocks and crags. The mare Judy whinnied in delight, but Hornsby's stockhorse laid back his ears and bared his teeth, He was a hardy old steed, thoroughly domesticated, and with no brumby in him, but the obvious challenge to fight, issued by the wild stallion on the rock, stirred even his ancient blood, though he had not the slightest intention of accepting the challenge.

"What a horse!" breathed Preston. "Wonder who owns him?

"Nobody, I'd say," replied Hornsby. "He's a wild brumby. Gosh, what I'd give to own him, Norm!"

"Me too. What are we waiting for? Let's take after him!" said the excited Preston, and Hornsby laughed loudly.

"Break it down, Norm," he begged. "What chance do you think we would have, chasing a brumby among the mountains on our old nags? The only way to catch that beauty would be to lure him into a trap. Anyway, you can bet he is not on his own. If I know anything of brumbies, he's with a band and you can bet your last sock that he is the leader."

As if to endorse that statement, the black stallion issued another high-pitched and defiant challenge, which caused another wave of ecstasy to run through the feminine Judy, while the old stockhorse again bared his ancient teeth.

Blackie surveyed the scene below for a few seconds more and then withdrew from sight. Back in the scrub his band was grazing and he rejoined them. He had now been the leader for more than a year and was fully grown, wild and proud. It was the first time he had been in this country, though settlers and squatters further north had had cause to curse his presence.

Though he did not possess the daring of his father, having inherited a lot of his mother's gentle disposition, nobody could teach him anything about raiding settlements and kicking down fences to release station-bred horses or to ravage growing crops.

Down in the gully, Preston and Hornsby were still discussing him.

"I'd like to take a couple of days off and see what I could do about that horse," said Hornsby. "How about coming out tomorrow and bringing Black Herbie with us? He knows more about horses than the rest of us put together."

"Suits me if the boss will let us," said Preston.

"I'm going to try to scale up to that rock and see if I can catch another glimpse of the beauty," said Hornsby. "I wouldn't mind betting it was old Bushranger himself."

Preston shook his head in doubt.

"I don't think so. Why, it must be getting on to five years since he was last around these parts. I've heard tales from other places about him and his band, but he has never been here since he stole Margaret."

"It is a wonder he has survived so long with everyone out to catch him," remarked Hornsby.

"I doubt if he has. You can't believe everything you hear. If Bushranger is still alive he'll be a very old horse. Brumbies don't live to a great age in their wild state, especially stallions. The young 'uns kill off the old hands," said Preston.

"True enough. Well, are you going to scale up that rock with me to see what we can see?"

Preston shook his head lazily. "Haven't got the energy," he confessed. "Anyway, that cliff looks mighty stiff to me."

"I'll give it a go," said Hornsby, and did so.

He was lucky to find a rather easy way up the cliff face. Jutting roots of trees, projecting rocks and deep pockets provided him with the necessary foot and hand-holds. It was not a very great height to climb, but it was rugged enough to make him pant long before he reached the rock on which Blackie had stood.

Reaching it, he paused for a moment to wipe his face with a large coloured handkerchief. Then he looked around him. A faint track at the base of the rock which sloped gently to the ground caught his eye. It wound out of sight among the trees and appeared to lead downwards towards the flat country. Obviously it had often been used by brumbies, and Hornsby wondered why their presence in these hills had not been reported before to the Sylvester homestead.

"See anything?" Preston bawled up at him.

"Only bush and rocks, but there is a brumby pad right here," Hornsby yelled back.

"Going to follow it?"

"You can bet it leads to the flat, so I won't trouble. Be with you in a minute or two."

But it was all of five minutes before Hornsby again reached the waiting Preston. The climb down had been as hard as the upward scramble.

"This wants looking into," said Hornsby as he dusted the sand and dirt from his clothes. "If this gully runs out on to the level country, and I'm sure it does, we might be able to work something. By the look of that pad up there, the brumbies use it a fair bit. We won't disturb them now, but will have a look at the country round here. If we could block this gully somehow, we might be able to drive those horses into a trap."

"If they stay long enough," said Preston doubtfully.

"Quite so. We will have to get a move on. I'll put it up to the boss tonight."

Remounting, the two men rode slowly and cautiously along the gully. When they neared the spot where it opened out on to the flat, they dismounted.

"It might be a good idea, Norm, if one of us were to stay here with the horses and keep them quiet while the other takes a look at the flat," said Hornsby. "If the brumbies are down feeding and we barge out and they see us, they'll be off like the wind."

Preston agreed to stay with the stockhorses and prevent them from making noises which might alarm the brumbies, while his friend spied out the land.

Hornsby made his way cautiously to the end of the gully, keeping in cover behind bushes and trees as he went. When he reached the gully mouth, he dropped behind a bush and peered through the leaves and branches.

His pulse leaped and his heart thrilled at what he saw. About a quarter of a mile away, in the open country, was a mob of wild horses. The stockman counted fourteen. They were of most known horse colours, but what attracted him was the magnificent leader. He was grazing like the rest and seemed oblivious, or contemptuous, of danger.

"What a horse!" breathed Hornsby.

It was some time before he could tear himself away from the spot. Then he made his cautious way back to Preston and told him what he had seen.

"I'll bet the boss will be interested in all this," he finished.

"Do you think that horse is Bushranger? "

"No, I do not," said Hornsby. "I saw Bushranger once or twice and though this horse is mighty like him, he has a white blaze on his forehead and one white stocking on his left hind leg. Bushranger was completely black. Also, this chap is about three or four years old. If Bushranger is still alive, he'd be about nine or ten."

"White blaze and white stocking?" pondered Preston. "Doesn't that remind you of another black horse we used to know?"

"Huh? Another black horse?" pondered Hornsby and then slapped his thigh.

"Of course!" he exclaimed. "Margaret!"

"Exactly. Margaret, the girl that Bushranger stole."

"Why, that horse out there could be Bushranger's son!" ejaculated Hornsby.

"Could be? I'll bet my last sock that it is! Wait until we tell old Sylvester this! He'll be out here himself like a shot out of a gun!"

"Too right he will," grinned Hornsby. "Come on, let's get a move on for home."

It was nearly dark when they reached the homestead, but they wasted no time telling the squatter their news. Mr. Sylvester was deeply interested.

"Margaret's son, eh? Yes, it could be. Fancy that. All right, boys, I give you permission to go out and catch the animal if you can. He is yours if you succeed," he said.

Hornsby looked bewildered. "But, boss, if that brumby is the son of your mare Margaret, he rightly belongs to you," protested the stockman.

"Don't want him. Don't want to have any truck with brumbies. Don't like the things. Only good brumby is a dead one," grunted the squatter. "You catch this fellow, he's yours."

"Just as you say, boss, and thanks," said Hornsby, pleased, but still a little bewildered.

Early on the following morning, four horsemen left the station and rode swiftly towards the country where they hoped to find Blackie and his band. Hornsby was slightly in the lead, followed by Preston, Black Herbie and young George Sylvester. The lad had begged hard to be included in the party and his father had let him go.

"If he makes a nuisance of himself, Harry, shoot him straight back home," old Sylvester said to Hornsby.

"I'll do that, boss, but I don't think he will," laughed the stockman.

"He may be a lot of use to us."

"Of course I will. I'm always useful," said George modestly. "You watch me."

"They'll have no time to watch you, my lad," said his father. "Harry is your boss today and you do what he tells you, do you hear?"

"Yes, Dad," said George submissively.

When the party entered the gully in which Hornsby and Preston had been resting when they first sighted Blackie on the overhead rock, they dismounted to plan their campaign. Hornsby explained the layout of the country.

"At this time of the morning the brumbies will probably be up in the hills," he said. "Their track down to the flat runs near the entrance to this gully. As you know, we came in here through that break in the cliffs just back there. If that break were blocked up, this gully would make a fine trap because there is only one other outlet—at the start of the flat. Get the brumbies inside and block the flat entrance and they'll never get out."

"It sounds easy as you say it, but I can see a lot of hard work," said Preston doubtfully.

"Isn't it worth it?" demanded Hornsby. "If we can trap the whole band and break in the best of them, we'll make a lot of money. Anyway, the first thing to do is to make a strong barrier across the gap we came through."

"I reckon the first thing to do is to find out if the brumbies are still up in the hills. If they are gone we'd have a lot of work for nothing," said George.

"Good for you, George," applauded Hornsby. "How would you like to go scouting for them?"

George said he would like it very much, so, having obtained a few directions from Hornsby, he mounted Ginger and rode off down the gully towards the flats. When he reached the entrance, he dismounted and tied Ginger to a sapling. With caution, he stole forward to have a look at the place where the two stockmen, on the previous day, had seen the brumbies grazing. There was now no sign of them. "I hope they are still up in the hills," he said to himself.

He had no difficulty in finding the brumby pad. It opened on to the flat from between a narrow cleft in a huge rock wall. This cleft would permit only one horse at a time to pass through. George went through it and fallowed the track upwards. It was not hard going, because the wild horses had picked their way with care, avoiding rocks, trees, pitfalls and other obstructions, winding in and out of the scrub.

He had gone about half a mile when he heard a horse whinny. Quickly withdrawing behind a tree, he waited until the sound was repeated and then, peering round the tree trunk, he caught a brief glimpse of something moving. Cautiously he crept forward and, parting some thick bushes, gazed out on to a clearing in which there were grazing about a dozen horses, including Blackie.

Horse lover that he was, the magnificent appearance of the black stallion filled him with admiration, but he did nothing to disturb the peaceful scene. Instead, he withdrew quietly and stole back the way he had come. As soon as he reached the flat again, he secured Ginger and rode back to his three comrades who were already hard at work cutting down saplings to form a barrier across the gap.

When he told Hornsby what he had seen, the stockman made a prompt decision.

"Go back to the flat, George, and stay there near the pad," he said. "If Blackie and his friends start to come down, hunt them back again. It should be easy if only one at a time can come through that cleft you mention. We must keep them in the hills until we are ready for them. We've got to complete this barrier and then make a gate for the entrance at the flat."

"Which will take a week to do and Blackie and his band might escape one night," objected Preston.

"You're right, Norm," said Hornsby after a moment's thought. "Looks as if we'll have to camp on the job."

"The boss won't like that. He can't afford to have us out here for a week. There is work to be done at the station, you know. The boss doesn't like brumbies all that much," said Preston.

The four then sat down to plan the thing out again. They could think of no solution until George remarked, "why not wait until the band is out on the plains and then just chase Blackie and run him down?"

"On what horses?" asked Preston scornfully.

"Dad's thoroughbreds."

"I can see your old man lending us his thoroughbreds to chase brumbies," said Hornsby, adding, "I don't think!" He got to his feet. "Let us go and have a look at the brumby pad where it reaches the level ground. We might get some sort of inspiration on the spot."

Leaving their horses where they were, the four walked the half mile to the entrance of the gully. The pad dropped to the flat about fifty yards to the left.

When Black Herbie inspected the narrow opening between the rocks, he got excited.

"Get up on top of rock there," he said, pointing skywards. "Drop rope round brumby's neck as he goes through."

"Hey?" ejaculated Hornsby, "and get dragged down on top of him!"

"Tie rope round tree up there," said Herbie.

"Could be done, maybe," said Hornsby thoughtfully. "Let us go up there and have a look around."

Passing through the cleft in single file, the three men and the boy ascended the slope and came out on top of the rock overlooking the cleft below.

"H'm, it might be possible. Tie one end of the rope to that tree there, lie on this rock and when Blackie passes down below, rope him. Have a longish rope so that he can get out of the narrow passage, and we have him," mused Hornsby.

It was decided that Black Herbie as the most expert rope thrower in the party should be the one to try to capture the wild horse. The party would linger in the vicinity until sundown to make certain that the band did not come down earlier.

"When I was up the track this morning," said George, "I noticed a couple of places where a person might hide and not be seen by the brumbies. I reckon it would be a good idea if I were to find a place up there where I could signal to Herbie on his rock here. As soon as I saw the horses coming, I could wave to him and it would give him a minute or two to prepare."

"No doubt about it, George has all the brains today," said Hornsby. "Off you go, lad, and see what you can do."

So George went up the brumby pad until he came to a rock surrounded by trees and foliage. He could see a hundred yards up the pad when hidden behind bushes, while to the rear he could discern Herbie, Hornsby and Preston on the rock overlooking the cleft. He lay down on his stomach, turned on his side so that he could see his companions, and waved his hand. They waved back. He then scrambled down and returned to them.

"That's that fixed. All we can do now is to wait," said Preston. "We'll do it in the gully. It may be hours before the brumbies get a move on."

"In the meantime, one of us had better ride back to the homestead and get a couple of good, long, strong ropes. What we have with us won't be good enough," said Hornsby.

Preston volunteered to go. The ride there and back would not take more than an hour at the outside. "Tell Dad we'll be bringing Blackie home with us tonight," George shouted as the stockman rode off.

"Optimist!" shouted back the laughing Preston.

There was little that the waiting trio could do until Preston returned. Black Herbie volunteered to keep sentry watch on the cleft and departed. Hornsby and George sat in the shade of a tree and yarned. Preston was back well within the expected period, bringing several stout ropes, calculated to hold the strongest horse.

"I think we'd better take up our positions now," said Hornsby as the sun sank lower in the west. "We'll take the horses down near the gully entrance so that they'll be handy if needed."

When they reached the flat entrance and had secured their horses, Hornsby instructed George to take up his position on his spy rock while Herbie mounted that overlooking the cleft.

"As soon as you get George's signal, Herbie, you prepare for action. Norman and I will stay hidden near the entrance. If you manage to rope Blackie hang on to him for dear life. Norm and I will try to rope him too. With three of us hanging on, he can't escape."

"Righto, Harry," said George, while Herbie nodded his agreement.

The aboriginal stockman and George parted company on the rise, George to proceed up the brumby pad and the blackfellow to take up a position on his particular rock. He was armed with the long rope, which had a running noose in it. He secured the free end to a large gum tree and after having shaken out the kinks at the lassoo end, lay down on his stomach, his head turned so that he could watch George who he could plainly see on his rock up the pad. Hornsby and Preston were concealed somewhere down below.

The time passed slowly as time will when one is eagerly waiting for a cherished event. Over an hour crept by before Black Herbie became alert. He had seen George wave his hand. The brumbies were coming! Instantly the aboriginal stockman rolled on his stomach and got his lassoo ready. The horses would never think of looking upwards, so there was little fear of detection.

Turning his head sideways, he caught a brief glimpse of the oncoming wild horses, Blackie in the lead. They were proceeding slowly in single file.

A bend in the track took Blackie out of sight, but Herbie was ready. Neatly judging the time, he raised himself slightly and peered over the edge of the rock. Blackie was just entering the gap in the rocks and appeared to be quite unaware of possible danger.

Gently the stockman lowered the noose and, as Blackie was almost directly beneath, dropped it. His aim was perfect. The noose dangled in front of the brumby's nose and he walked straight into it. The noose was around Blackie's neck before he was aware of it.

Herbie did not pull on the rope as Blackie walked on shaking his head. When the noose began to tighten, Herbie quickly took in the slack and then gently began paying out the rope to its full length. Then he held on to it tightly and braced himself for the coming struggle.

Blackie, now aware of the menace, stopped dead. Then he plunged forward, nearly choking himself. Whirling round so that he was facing the rocks, he stood on his hind legs as if he were climbing into the air. Down he came, his hard hoofs striking sparks from the stones, and while the rest of his band poured through the narrow passage and scattered in all directions, the black stallion fought the thing that held him. He screamed and squealed, pawed the air, bucked, lay down and rolled over, but the strong rope held fast.

With an excited whoop, Hornsby dashed from cover whirling his lassoo. Blackie twisted his head to see this new menace, and hampered though he was by the rope, reared on his hind legs, intending to crush this human intruder if he came within range. The wily stockman, however, coolly watched his chance and his rope snaked out unerringly, to catch the brumby round one leg. Hornsby ran in a circle and as the brumby's hoofs hit the ground, gave a tug on the rope and Blackie fell on his chest and then on his nose.

He lay on the ground for a moment or two, panting heavily, and then got another shock as a third rope assailed him. Preston had dropped his noose over Blackie's head.

Held by two ropes round his neck and one round his leg, the wild horse was helpless. Hornsby and Preston hung on to their ropes while Black Herbie saw that the one he had was kept taut. It was long enough to keep the horse clear of the rocks against which he might take a fancy to dash himself.

Young George, whooping with excitement, joined Herbie on the rock overlooking the cleft.

"George!" Hornsby yelled, "go and get our horses. Be as quick as you can. We may not be able to hold this beauty for long."

George slid off the rock, passed down through the cleft and ran into the gully. He was back within minutes, riding Ginger and leading the other three horses. Blackie was still lying on the ground, two ropes round his neck and one wound round a front leg. He had tried several times to rise, but had not succeeded.

Leaving his rope secured to the tree, Black Herbie came down to the flat and mounted his horse. Hornsby threw him the end of the rope he was holding and ran to mount his own steed. As soon as he was in the saddle, Preston threw him his rope.

"Ease your rope, Herbie, so that he can get up," Hornsby directed. "I'll try to shake my rope free of his leg. When that is done, Herbie's rope and the one tied to the tree will hold him until I can get mine round his neck. Let's go."

The manoeuvre came off as planned. As soon as the rope held by Black Herbie was allowed to slacken, the one tied to the tree eased. Blackie tried to heave himself to his feet, and as he did so, Hornsby allowed his rope to drop down. This permitted Blackie to stand up. He shook his foreleg vigorously and the noose loosened and fell to the ground. He kicked it free and Hornsby quickly wound it in, shook out the kinks, reopened the noose and before Blackie knew what was going on, had deftly thrown it around his neck.

The brumby now had three ropes around his neck, two held by men on horses and one tied to a tree up the hillside.

"George," shouted Hornsby, "get up there and free that rope. Throw it down to Norm. Norm, you grab it and get on your horse. Herbie and I will hold him until then. With three of us hanging on, we'll get him back to the station all right. We'll let him have his head. I'll ride to the right, Herbie to the left, both slightly in front, and Norm behind. If he doesn't run home, we'll drag him there. It will be just like the spokes on a wheel. Our ropes will be the spokes and Blackie will be the hub."

Once again the carefully thought-out plan succeeded. George freed the rope from the tree and tossed the end down to Preston who was already mounted. The stockman caught it deftly.

Blackie, of course, was not taking all this lying down. As Herbie and Hornsby hung on like grim death, the brumby reared and bucked and plunged, rolled on the ground, stood up and pawed the air and did everything he could think of to free his neck of the maddening ropes. He did not succeed. He was a magnificent horse and most powerful, but he could not compete with the combined strength of the three men and their stockhorses.

By skilful handling, they managed to get him turned into the gully. Blackie made a slash up it, but was brought to a stumbling walk by the three restraining ropes. When they reached the gap in the cliffs through which they had entered the gully the brumby went through of his own volition, closely followed by the three rope holders, with George in the rear. It was fortunate that the gap was a wide one, or there might have been trouble.

They were now out in the open paddocks, and the rest was comparatively easy. Blackie ran like the wind, but the others matched him, letting him have his head most of the time, but keeping the ropes taut enough to remind him that he was a prisoner.

It was a wild ride across country to the homestead, but they made it. Every time Blackie tried to veer from the course, one of the riders manipulated his rope to make the black stallion change his direction, if not his mind. He could not double back, because the two men on either side restrained him, and in any case Preston was behind to check any such tendency to retreat.

They got him to the station yard in this fashion and there they held him until George could open the gate. Blackie refused to enter, so, executing an encircling movement, Herbie and Hornsby rode round him and into the enclosure and then literally dragged him through. Preston threw down his rope, George slammed the gate with a whoop of triumph and Blackie the brumby was a prisoner!

CHAPTER IV.
GEORGE DISOBEYS ORDERS

OLD John Sylvester leaned over the rail of the stockyard and looked thoughtfully at Blackie. That proud animal, his neck arched, was looking over the top rail on the opposite side and seemed to be as deep in thought as the squatter.

Blackie had the yard to himself and had done so ever since he had been at the station, which was now almost a month. After he had been broken in by Black Herbie, he had been turned into a paddock with some stockhorses, but his behaviour had been such that Mr. Sylvester had ordered that he be kept separate from all other horses on the station.

The brumby did not like the station horses and he showed his dislike with his hoofs and teeth. He had been used to homage and respect and he did not get it from the domesticated steeds. They had as little use for him as he had for them and there was nothing but fights, damaged fences and displays of bad temper in the paddock.

Since Blackie had been given his own yard, however, a change had come over him. He did not possess the wild, savage nature of his father; in fact he was rather a friendly soul, especially towards humans.

Harry Hornsby joined the squatter at the yard fence and the

older man remarked, "I don't like brumbies as you know, Harry, but that Blackie is a mighty fine horse. You know as much about horses as I do, but an extra word of advice won't come amiss, eh?"

"What you don't know about horses, nobody else knows, boss," said Hornsby, and the squatter smiled at the compliment.

"Whatever you do, Harry, don't mollycoddle him," he said. "That horse has had a tough upbringing, and you keep him tough. It is one of his finest qualities. Treat him right and he'll treat you right. Make a mate of him and it will repay you. Almost any wild creature can be tamed with kindness."

"That's a fact, boss," nodded the stockman. "Blackie and I are already good friends. But I can't see me mollycoddling him. How could anyone turn a horse like that into a sissy?"

"You don't understand what I mean," smiled the squatter. "That horse has good blood in him, and blood will tell. That is one fine quality he possesses, but he has more. Never forget that he has been born and bred on the plains and in the ranges. He has had to live, sometimes, on poor grass and precious little water. Don't mollycoddle him by giving him too much lucerne, corn and oats to eat if there is grass about, and don't let him drink water unless he actually needs it. He has built up his qualities of endurance on short rations, and you never know, in these wild days, when you'll have need of a fast horse which can stand the pace."

"That's sound argument, boss," nodded Hornsby.

"Of course it is. Different horses need different treatment. You take a racehorse. He needs a certain amount of mollycoddling, such as a good stable, plenty of attention and the right tucker, but when a horse has a job of work to do, then it is different."

"You mean that I should treat Blackie as an ordinary stockhorse?"

"I don't say that you should always use him as a stockhorse, but you could do worse. Is there any horse tougher than the ordinary stockhorse?" demanded Sylvester.

"They are tough all right," agreed Hornsby.

"They have to be." The squatter broke off and had another look at Blackie, who was still deep in thought. The stallion was gazing away towards the ranges and wishing that he was back there with his old band of faithful followers and not cooped up in a place where the horses were either ignorant clods or pampered sissies.

"Yes, stockhorses are tough," repeated old Sylvester. "We ride them all day and if we are camping, we just turn them loose for the night without rubbing them down or cleaning them up. If they're good campers and won't stray, we forget about them until morning. If we think they'll stray, we shove hobbles on them and leave them to look after themselves. At home we put them in the paddock after we've taken the saddle off them, and let them rip. They find their own grass and water unless there's a drought on."

"I've known plenty of stockhorses that have never been shod, never been in a stable in their lives and wouldn't know what corn was if you shoved it under their noses, yet any one of them will work day in and day out, chasing stock, travelling over good and bad country and thinking nothing of covering two or three hundred miles a week; and they do it all on grass," said Hornsby.

"The climate has a lot to do with it," said Sylvester. "Horses are like sheep. They prefer a dry climate."

"I might make a racehorse out of him," mused the stockman.

"You could do worse than that. You've ridden him a lot and have gained his confidence, but use him for stock work for a time and see how he goes," the squatter advised.

"But whatever you do, Harry, keep a close eye on him. He'd be a first class mount for a bushranger," he said meaningly. "They haven't been in this part of the country yet, but there is no telling when they might decide to pay us a visit."

Harry Hornsby nodded. He knew that what the squatter said was only too true. The bushrangers needed the fastest and best horses they could get, and in the districts they infested, it was almost impossible for any person to keep a really valuable horse. Special raids were organised by horse thieves and it was nothing for them to travel a hundred miles in order to steal an animal that had made a name for itself as a racer. The story of Blackie had spread through the district and secret friends of the bushrangers were sure to pass on any information to them.

"Every time I look at that horse, I see Margaret," said old Mr. Sylvester, breaking in on the stockman's reverie. "You wouldn't think that a stallion could look so much like his mother. Of course, Blackie is stronger and more powerfully built, but he is the image of his mother in other ways."

"Yes, he is good-tempered enough, but still a little bit of a fire-eater," said Hornsby.

"Just high spirits, Harry, just high spirits," said the squatter. "There is no vice in the horse. If any should develop, don't blame it on to Margaret, but on to that Bushranger animal."

"Black Herbie knocked out of him any vice he might have had," said Hornsby. "He's an absolute marvel with horses, that man."

"He is. I thought Blackie might prove too much for him, but he tamed him all right. I'll never forget that day when Herbie took him in hand!"

"Nor me, either," said Hornsby, and both men smiled at the recollection.

The breaking in of Blackie had been an event at the station. From the moment the black stockman had made his first move until he had handed the broken horse over to Hornsby, there had not been a dull moment. Herbie had his own breaking-in methods and they were most efficient and thorough. When, with Hornsby's assistance, he had roped and tied Blackie, shoved a saddle on him and a bit in his mouth, the brumby was never out of his power. Such an exhibition of buckjumping followed, that even the station hands, hardened as they were to seeing horses broken in, marvelled at the horsemanship of the aboriginal.

Having survived the worst of the bucking, the rolling, the pawing and the numerous other methods Blackie employed to get rid of the man on his back, Black Herbie had the gate of the yard flung open. Urging the brumby into the wide open spaces, he had given him his head. The wild horse went for long miles at a breakneck gallop and Herbie kept him up to it. They were away all day and when they returned, Blackie had been ridden to a standstill and had hardly the energy to drag one foot after another.

This routine was followed exactly for three days, at the end of which Blackie was a beaten horse. He had been conquered and man was his master.

"You still don't cotton to brumbies, boss," remarked Hornsby with a smile.

"I do not. If I did, you wouldn't be owning Blackie."

"You're not regretting having given him to me, are you, boss?" the stockman asked, a little anxiously.

"Not in the least. He's yours for keeps. I like the horse. He's a fine animal, but he's got the brumby in him and that stops me from actually loving him."

"If everybody thought the same as you, boss, the story writers would starve to death like cows in the desert," grinned Hornsby.

"I don't quite get the meaning of that," replied old Sylvester with a frown.

"Well, boss, you do a lot of reading, and I thought you must have come across a lot of stories with the same old plot. You know, the daughter runs away from home and is never seen again, then her son returns to the old homestead and is covered with kisses and kindness by his old grandparents who miss his mother."

"You're as mad as a halfpenny watch, Hornsby," said the squatter with an indignant snort. "If you expect me to climb this fence and kiss that big black brumby on the nose because he is the son of one of my favourite mares, you want to get your head examined."

"Yes, boss," said the stockman, and roared with laughter, the old man joining in.

"Anyway, we can't stay here all day admiring Blackie," he said at last. "I've got work to do, even if my men have not."

"Yes, boss," replied Hornsby, taking the hint with a smile.

When Mr. Sylvester entered the house, he went straight to his private office to do work which was essential, but which he hated—bookkeeping. He was alone in the house except for his old aboriginal housekeeper who was pottering around somewhere, and he was rather sorry for it. He would have welcomed the presence of young George, who was away herding sheep, or of a visitor—anyone who would give him the excuse to put off for a little longer the task of going through his books.

He was idly turning the pages of a ledger when young George came in. The lad was covered with dust and, throwing his hat untidily on the floor, sank into a chair and sighed.

"What goes on?" demanded his father. "How many times have I told you to wipe your feet before you come into the house? Get up out of that armchair, too, my lad. Dash it, you're dirt from head to foot. Do you think I've got nothing to do but keep this place clean after you turn it into a dustheap?"

George grinned.

"What about Hettie, Dad?" he asked. "Have you sacked her?"

Hettie was the aboriginal housekeeper who did the minimum amount of work in the maximum amount of time and did it very badly.

"Don't talk to me about Hettie," said the squatter disgustedly. "Haven't I sacked her a thousand times? Haven't I told her to get back to her tribe and stop there? What has she done about it?"

"Nothing," said George.

"Exactly. She spends all her life doing that," snorted his father.

"By the way, what brings you home at this hour?" he asked. "I thought you were supposed to be out helping Black Herbie round up that bunch of sheep in the northern paddock? Don't tell me you have finished already, because I won't believe you."

"Yes, Dad," replied the boy with a sigh. "We didn't have too many to round up. Only twenty-seven. They're all in the yard down the bottom, ready to be shorn."

"Hey, only twenty-seven? Where are the others?" demanded the squatter. "Too lazy to bring them in?"

"No, Dad, we could have brought them in," said George carefully, "but it would have been hard work and I don't think they would have been much use to us as they were."

"Son," said old Sylvester impatiently, "what the devil are you shilly-shallying about? Why didn't you bring them all in?"

"Dingoes."

"Dingoes?" echoed his father. "What do you mean dingoes?"

"Dad," said George slowly, "we used to own a little mob of fifty sheep. Now we have only twenty-seven. The dingoes got the rest of them. Their bodies are scattered all over the paddock."

"Bless my heart and soul, if it's not one thing it's another!" stormed the squatter. "Thank goodness I'm not a sheep man but only keep a few for rations. Dingoes, hey? Well, son, don't sit there looking the picture of misery! Get out and tell Black

Herbie to do something about it. Set traps, set poison baits, get a gun and shoot them…"

He stopped short and eyed his son.

"What's biting you, George?" he demanded. "There's no need to look so sick about it. These things happen. It's a heavy loss, but we'll survive. Why are you sitting there looking like a dying duck in a sandstorm? I never knew you were so attached to sheep! Now, had the dingoes killed off a few horses, I could understand you looking so downhearted."

George shook his head.

"I'm not concerned about the sheep, Dad," he confessed.

"I'm sorry we lost them, of course, and I'll help Herbie go after the dingoes. It's not that."

"Well, what is it?"

George wrestled with himself mentally for a moment, and then, "I've had a row with Harry Hornsby," he burst out.

"What over?"

"Blackie."

"What about Blackie? Come on, lad, out with it. I haven't got all day to waste trying to answer your riddles," said his father impatiently.

"Dad, why can't I have a ride on Blackie?" exclaimed the boy. "Harry won't let me. He says I can't ride well enough, and that Blackie is too wild for me to handle. It isn't true. Blackie isn't wild any more and I'm as good a rider as Harry Hornsby is, any day in the week."

"We won't go into all this again, George," said the squatter. "I've told you before that Blackie belongs to Harry and if he says you can't ride the horse, then you can't. So you stop pestering him and stop pestering me. As a matter of fact, my boy, do you think it is the square thing to do, coming to your father behind Harry's back and trying to make me overrule my stockman? That is almost as bad as carrying tales. So cut it out."

"I'm sorry, Dad, I didn't think of that. But I'm a good rider. I wouldn't harm the horse and Blackie and I are good pals. Couldn't you get round Harry to let me have a ride?"

"No, and that's that. Apart from the fact that Harry owns the horse and is the only person with the right to say who should ride him, I don't think you could handle Blackie. He's still wild."

"I'm a good rider, Dad."

"You are, son, a very good rider. All the same, keep off Blackie. I'm sure Harry is only thinking of your welfare. It would not be nice for him, or for any of us, if you came a cropper and injured yourself riding that black villain."

"All right, Dad," said George submissively. "I'll go and see Herbie about laying those baits and traps for the dingoes."

"Do that, and forget about Blackie for a while. You may get a chance to ride him later."

Young George wandered out of the house and down to the yard where Blackie was confined. He leaned over the rail and looked fondly at the big black horse.

"I'll ride you yet, mate," he confided to Blackie, who pricked up his ears and regarded the boy benevolently. He knew George as a friendly soul. Many a yarn they had had together unknown to Harry Hornsby or George's father. The brumby might be a little proud and standoffish with others, but not with George.

He had been standing in the middle of the yard when George arrived, and presently he minced a proud way over to the rail and stretched out his head. His nostrils quivered as George gently stroked his forehead. A nice lad, thought Blackie.

It was not the first time by any means that George and Blackie had communed together. George had won the big horse's confidence without anyone else knowing. With thistles and carrots and sometimes apples and potatoes he had wooed and won the brumby, but he had never yet entered the yard itself.

Glancing swiftly around and seeing that nobody was near, George took his courage in both hands, slipped through the rails and approached the horse. Blackie regarded him with a kindly eye and did not object when George patted his neck and ran his hand down the side of his shoulder. Encouraged, the boy patted him on the flank and then put his arm round his neck. Blackie took it all in good part, in fact he gave a slight whinny of pleasure.

"You beauty!" said the boy softly. Blackie nickered as if in complete agreement, and rubbed his head against George's shirt front.

"You don't hate yourself, do you Blackie?" asked the lad and Blackie nickered again.

When he climbed back through the rails, the stallion leaned over and made noises with his lips. He seemed sorry that George had left the yard.

"I don't care what Dad or Harry Hornsby say, I'm going to ride you one day, Blackie," he told the horse. "How do you feel about that?"

As if in concurrence, Blackie nodded his head vigorously and then trotted to the other side of the yard.

Going in search of Black Herbie, George found him in the harness shed and told him what his father had said about the dingoes.

"We've got to lay baits and set traps," said George.

"We do," replied the aboriginal briefly. "Not today. Too busy."

It was on the following morning that young George got his big chance. Old Sylvester decided to go with Harry Hornsby and Herbie to the sheep paddock to inspect the damage caused by the dingoes and to supervise the laying of the baits. They would be away most of the morning and probably part of the afternoon and George was instructed to stay at the homestead and make himself useful doing family chores.

The lad did a few odd jobs, but his mind was not on work. Presently he left the house and wandered down to the yard to have a yarn with Blackie. The black horse greeted him with a welcome whinny. George slipped through the rails and as he fondled the brumby with one hand, presented him with an apple with the other. Blackie accepted it gravely.

"Blackie," said George, "keep this to yourself, but I'm going to ride you some day."

He broke off as a daring idea entered his mind.

"And by Jingo I will, right now!" he exclaimed. "Wait there!"

It was a silly remark, because Blackie had nowhere to go and could not have gone anywhere of his own volition had he wanted to.

George slipped out of the yard and ran to the harness shed where his saddle and bridle were kept. As he took them down he told himself, "I'll go only for a short ride. I won't be away more than ten minutes. Nobody will be any the wiser."

From the house he heard a strange, rather unearthly row proceeding, but that did not worry him. It was merely Hettie's particular brand of singing, and indicated that she was raiding the food cupboard. Hettie always sang, or made noises which she fondly believed to be singing, when she was pilfering food. Both George and his father knew of this, but did nothing about it. After all, the old girl did not eat very much.

Feeling safe from detection by the black housekeeper, George opened the yard gate and closed it behind him. As he approached Blackie with the saddle and bridle, he felt a little apprehensive. The horse had been ridden by Hornsby plenty of times, but Hornsby had been his sole rider to date. Added to that, the stockman had been the only person to saddle and bridle the black horse apart from the initial breaking-in period by Black Herbie.

George, approaching warily, was prepared for trouble, but

Blackie looked at him benevolently. Nor did the horse object as the boy gently slipped the bit into his mouth and threw the saddle on his back. He did flinch a little as George tightened the girth strap, but the lad's most anxious moment came when he prepared to mount. He placed a foot in the stirrup, his heart in his mouth. Then, breathing a soft prayer, he vaulted lightly into the saddle and tensed himself for trouble. There wasn't any.

Gently he turned the big black stallion towards the gate and Blackie went willingly. At the gate, George dismounted, led Blackie through, shut the gate, and remounted. Blackie acted like a lamb.

George trotted him out of the yard and towards the track that led away across the open paddocks. When he was well out of range of the homestead, he gave a wild whoop and headed across country at a fast canter.

CHAPTER V.
BLACKIE CHANGES HANDS

ABOUT three miles from the homestead on the bank of a small creek, there lived in a bark and bag humpy an old retired swagman and shearer, who was a friend of George's, and the lad decided to pay him a visit.

There were some who said that this old man was mad that, living alone with not even a dog for company, had made him "queer." What his correct name was, nobody except himself knew, but everyone called him "old Fred."

George did not consider old Fred mad. The lad regarded him as good company, and many a time he had sat at the old chap's fire and listened enthralled to stories of the track and far distant places. When he was a swagman, old Fred had tramped the Outback shearing and doing other work, never staying long in any one place; but as the years passed one by one in endless procession, the time at length arrived when he grew too old to carry his swag the long miles between shearing sheds.

So old Fred decided to retire. He built himself the hut on the creek bank and settled down to end his days peacefully, earning enough money for his simple needs by tinkering—repairing pots and pans, boots and shoes, tubs and tanks, or anything else, for anyone who would give him work.

George smiled as he cantered along the track that led to the hut. He was thinking of what Harry Hornsby had said only the day before about old Fred.

"Of course the old chap is mad," the stockman had declared. "Why, he talks to the blessed birds all day long. He must be off his nut."

Old Fred was a great bird lover. George loved birds too, but he loved horses more. He looked forward eagerly to the surprise he would give old Fred when he turned up on Blackie. Old Fred, of course, had heard all about the brumby and was among those who had warned George to keep off the horse.

Nearing the hut, the lad was momentarily startled by a great din among the trees, and presently he came across a swarm of noisy birds that kicked up a terrific row as they flashed on swift wings through the bushes, now lingering to sip honey from a flower, then dashing wildly to another tree on which blossoms hung, chattering all the time. A stranger might have been pardoned for thinking that a vast bird war was in progress, but George knew better.

"Hullo, there, Micky," he called as a grey bird with black and white markings and yellow round the eyes flashed past close to Blackie's nose. Out of the scrub dashed a willie wagtail, making a harsh noise that sounded like, "yah-didja-didja-did." Without hesitation, Micky, the noisy miner, also known as the soldier bird, swerved round and dashed at the wagtail. That large-tailed bird suddenly decided that he had a pressing engagement elsewhere and fled through the thickets. It was not often that Willie turned tail, but he did so on this occasion, much to George's amusement.

Willie probably would not stop until he reached his own nest, where, in safety, he would tell his mate a highly imaginative story of how he had fought a soldier.

George laughed as he rode onwards. There were always flocks of birds around old Fred's hut.

As he came in sight of it he saw old Fred come to the door carrying a saucer. George hailed him and the old man shouted a return greeting.

"New horse you've got, George," said old Fred. "Fine looking beast, too. Had him long?"

"This," said George proudly, "is Blackie the brumby. I know you told me not to ride him, but I'm doing it and he's as quiet as a mouse."

"H'm, seems so," said old Fred. "However, you watch him. He's a brumby and you never know when you've got them."

"What have you got in that saucer, Fred?" asked the boy as he dismounted and tied Blackie to a tree limb.

"Something for that rascal, Micky Miner the soldier bird and his noisy mates," said old Fred.

"Why," said George, peering into the saucer, "it's honey!"

"Yes, and you'll see some fun in a minute."

There had been no sign of the soldier birds around the hut. The flock George had seen had apparently passed on; but hardly had the old swagman stepped back from the shelf he had built on a tree trunk for such gifts to the birds as honey, than a grey shadow flashed swiftly past and perched beside the saucer. It was Micky the miner. He chattered noisily, then dipped his beak into it, held back his head to swallow, and then dipped again.

"Enough to make him sick," said old Fred. "At least he'd get sick if he ate it all, but he won't. You'll see!"

After a few sips of the free honey, Micky dashed away, chirping and chattering. Whatever he said must have excited his friends, for they came in a small cloud, all trying to land on the shelf at once. This was impossible, so the bystanders enjoyed the spectacle of three or four birds trying to gobble the honey while a pile of others fluttered over or stood on their backs, making a terrific din as if they were all being killed.

"That's what I call real mateship," old Fred observed. "Plenty of birds would have eaten the whole issue. Not Micky. He goes and tells his cobbers and there they all are, fighting like Kilkenny cats, you'd think, but, in reality, as happy as they can be."

The chattering and fluttering went on for a long time until every drop of honey had vanished. Like all honeyeaters, the soldier birds had long split tongues and with these they licked the saucer clean. Then, after wheeling and calling around the hut as if they were thanking old Fred and asking for more on the morrow, they dashed away among the trees. Probably they would not be there next day, but far away, seeking more honey from distant bush blossoms.

"I wonder where they build their nests?" asked George. "I've often searched for honey-eaters' nests but have never found any."

"You'd need to go away back into the ranges," said old Fred. "I've only seen two in all my life and both were in quiet gullies far away from cattle and people. They make hanging nests in low bushes. They are rather shy birds at home, but noisy as anything in a mob. I've often run across them while on the track. They come around the camp and you can't get rid of them. I've never known such cheeky, inquisitive birds. They are worse than old women telling tales about their neighbours over back fences. They mind everybody's business but their own."

George could not help smiling a little at the old man's enthusiasm over his bird friends, but he appreciated Fred's kindly and simple nature.

"Well, I must be getting along, Fred," he said. "I'm going to ride into town and then back home."

"All right, George, but remember what I said. Be careful with that horse."

"I will," replied the boy as he mounted Blackie and, with a cheery hand wave, rode off.

As he cantered steadily along the bush track that led to the township, he felt as proud and happy as any bush lad, with a good horse under him, could be. Blackie, of course, enjoyed the outing, too. He hated being cooped up in his yard.

Rounding a slight bend in the track, George noticed another horseman trotting towards him. The new arrival was a young man of about twenty-three years of age, wearing a coloured shirt, moleskin pants tucked into high riding boots and a cabbage tree hat. George, who knew everybody in the district, had never seen him before.

The stranger reined in his horse and waited for George to reach him. The youngster called out a cheery, "Hullo, mate," and would have cantered past, but the stranger held up a hand for him to stop. George did so.

"Good day, young fellow," said the horseman pleasantly. "Can you tell me how far I am from Sylvester's station?"

"About two miles," replied George. "I've just come from there."

"Work at the place, huh?"

"In a sort of a way," smiled the lad. "I'm George Sylvester and my Dad owns the property."

"Does he now?" asked the stranger, eyeing the lad keenly. As he did so, George took stock of his horse. Not a bad type of animal, he considered. He was thinking along lines similar to the stranger, who said suddenly, "That's a pretty fine type of nag you're riding son."

"The best in this district," claimed George proudly.

"Yes. I guess he'll do me fine," said the stranger thoughtfully. "Wrap him up. I'll take him."

"Beg your pardon?" asked George, wondering what sort of obscure joke the stranger was cracking.

"I'll have that horse," said the man, looking straight at George.

"I don't understand you."

Slowly and deliberately, the strange horseman slid a hand inside his shirt, and when he withdrew it, the startled lad saw a pistol.

"Get down off that horse!" commanded the man.

"What?" ejaculated George.

"Look here, can't you understand plain Australian? I want that horse. Get off quick, or I'll blow you out of the saddle with this revolver. I mean business!"

"But—but..."

"No buts about it. Are you going to get off that horse or must I flatten you out?" roared the stranger, edging his own steed close to Blackie and shoving the muzzle of the pistol against young George's chest.

"You can't steal this horse, mister," protested the boy. "He doesn't belong to me."

"Doesn't he? You're young to be a horse thief, aren't you? I'll be doing you a good turn by relieving you of him. It would be nice, wouldn't it, if the police came along and caught you with a stolen nag."

"I didn't steal him. He belongs to a man who works for Dad."

"Listen, we've wasted enough time in yapping," growled the man. "Off you get. That horse is mine."

"You're a dashed bushranger," said George suddenly.

"There's brains for you!" said the stranger ironically. "Johnny Gibson, at your service!"

"Bert Wall's mate!" exclaimed George in some awe.

"Correct."

"Well, you aren't going to take this horse to go bushranging and sticking up stations and coaches with," said George with spirit.

"Youngster," said Gibson steadily, "I won't argue with you.

If you are not off that horse by the time I count three, I'm going to shoot."

"But that would be murder," said the boy fearfully. "I thought that none of Bert Wall's gang ever shot people."

"You're away behind the times," said Gibson. "Anyway, I won't shoot you. I'll shoot that horse and then neither of us will have him."

George Sylvester looked at him aghast. That any human being could even think of shooting a horse like Blackie was something he would not believe. Through his mind ran some of the stories he had heard about Johnny Gibson and Bert Wall. They were horse and cattle thieves, robbers of wayside travellers, and had bailed up more than one mail coach and lonely station homestead.

They were, of course, a pair of thorough-paced scoundrels, but of all the stories George had heard, none had ever contained a bad word for the outlaws as far as horses were concerned. Good horses meant everything to them. That being so, he did not think that Gibson would shoot Blackie.

Doubtfully, however, and with tears in his eyes, he slowly dismounted. Blackie turned his head and gave an inquiring neigh. George patted his mane.

"Goodbye, dear old Blackie," he said with a sob.

"Stop that whining and howling," commanded the bushranger. "Hand me those reins and then get a move on home. I'll lead him for the time being. And listen to me, young feller-me-lad. If you tell the traps about this, I'll ride over to your old man's place and blow his brains out, and yours too."

"The police will get you yet, Johnny Gibson, and when they do, you'll be hanged," exclaimed George.

"I'd like to see the trap that could catch me, especially now I've got this horse. Now, get a move on and keep your mouth shut."

George again patted Blackie, who could not get the drift

of things at all. Why was young George leaving him with this other fellow?

"Look after him, won't you, mister?" begged the lad. "Don't knock him about, or let him get shot, will you?"

"Don't you worry about that, son. I'll look after him. I'll ride him till I'm sick of him and then I'll turn him loose. He might find his way home again. Who knows? Well, I'm off. Don't forget what I told you about keeping away from the traps."

Leaving George standing on the side of the road, Gibson dug spurs into his horse and moved away, expecting Blackie to meekly trot after him. Blackie, however, had other ideas. He couldn't see why he should have to go anywhere with this fellow.

As the bushranger moved off, Blackie stood still and the reins were almost jerked out of Gibson's hand. He stopped and, turning his head angrily, swore at the black stallion. Blackie received the verbal attack calmly, but gave a shake of the head as if he did not approve of the language. The action again almost caused Gibson to lose the reins.

"Get a move on, you black villain!" he shouted, tugging the reins. Blackie gave a short neigh and dug his front hoofs into the ground, as stubborn as any mule.

"Better let him go, mister," said George. "He'll be no good to you, and if he gets his temper up he'll kill you."

"No horse has ever got the better of me yet," boasted the outlaw.

Dismounting, he walked slowly towards Blackie, winding in the reins as he did so. Young Sylvester, watching anxiously, expected the bushranger to make a sudden attack on the horse, but he didn't. Gibson knew horses and appreciated their ways.

"What's wrong, old boy?" he said softly, as, reaching Blackie's head, he gently stroked his satin nose. Blackie liked it, but was a little suspicious of the stranger's intentions. He knew that something was amiss, but could not determine what it was.

Blackie was a horse that reacted to kindness. His master, Harry Hornsby, was always kind. So was young George. In fact all the human beings with whom he had come in contact, were good folk—with the possible exception of Black Herbie, who had given him a torrid time. Still, he held no grudge against the aboriginal stockman—the man who had tamed him.

While these thoughts were idly passing through his brain, Gibson was still stroking him and saying soothing words. He couldn't be such a bad chap, thought the brumby. Perhaps he was a friend of Hornsby's and George's.

When he gave a low whinny, Gibson knew he had won the day. With a final pat, he went to his own horse and mounted, and when he rode off, Blackie trotted obediently behind him. George Sylvester, with a heavy heart, watched them disappear among the trees.

What should he do, he asked himself. Return to the station and face the storm, or try to get Blackie back? There was small hope of doing that by himself. What about the police?

"I'll go on into town and tell the troopers," he said aloud and without wasting further time, strode off. It was a long walk, but nothing to the sturdy bush boy.

Sergeant William Potts was alone in the police station when George burst in with his startling news.

"Mr. Potts, a bushranger bailed me up in the bush and stole Harry Hornsby's horse from me," he shouted, without any preliminary greeting.

"Hey?" ejaculated the sergeant. "What game is this you're playing, young Sylvester?"

"It's true, sergeant," said the lad. "I was riding into town on Blackie when this man came up on a horse and pulled out a revolver and made me get off Blackie and made me give Blackie to him and he said he'd blow my brains out and my father's too and..."

"Oh, starve the kangaroos, George, pull up and get your breath back!" said Potts. "Take it easy and tell me what this is all about. Be calm, lad!" But George found it hard to be calm. He continued to pour out his story in a rushing torrent of words and the sergeant had to let him go ahead. When the lad had finished and was panting for breath, Sergeant Potts questioned him closely.

"This is very serious, George," he said gravely. "Are you sure that this man is Johnny Gibson, the bushranger?"

"He said he was. I have never seen him before in my life."

"Of course it could be anybody," mused the sergeant. "A lot of flash young fellows these days use the names of bushrangers when they break the law and as far as we know, Wall and Gibson are still operating around the northern areas. But as nothing has been heard of them for some time, they may have decided to come down here for a change of scenery."

He turned to George.

"I'll get hold of Trooper Sinclair and we'll ride out to the scene of the theft and have a look around," he said. "Then we'll go to your father's place. I'd like to borrow Black Herbie. Unfortunately we have no black trackers stationed here at the moment."

He stood up and put on his uniform cap and as he did so, George asked, "Mr. Potts, can you lend me a horse? It's six or seven miles home and..."

"Yes, I'll lend you a police horse," smiled the sergeant. "You won't find him as good as the horse you lost, but he's got a good few gallops left in him. The whole trouble with the police is that we have to put up with any sort of horses while the bushrangers have only the best—they see to that!"

Within five minutes the trio was ready to leave and they cantered down the little main street together. It was an uneventful ride to the place where Gibson had taken Blackie from George.

The police troopers did not waste much time there, but proceeded on to the Sylvester property, George's heart getting closer to his boots as the distance lessened.

What on earth could he say to Harry Hornsby and what could he say to his father? There was sure to be a frightful row about it! He had taken Blackie without permission and the horse had been stolen. He'd catch it hot, he was certain.

CHAPTER VI.
SCHOOL INTERLUDE

AS he had anticipated, George Sylvester did catch it hot from his father, but the punishment was such that he had never dreamed of—banishment for a month to the home of his Aunt Bertha, who lived in a town fifty miles from the Sylvester station.

Aunt Bertha was a kindly old lady who treated George well. The lad could do as he liked, but he was forbidden to ride horses and he had to go to the school in town. George did not mind the school so much, but he did miss his horse, Ginger.

As he sat in his aunt's kitchen eating his tea, his thoughts turned to that terrible day, two weeks ago, when he arrived home with Potts and Sinclair to break the news of the loss of Blackie and the saddle and bridle. How his father had raved and stormed! How Harry Hornsby had kicked up a row! His father had threatened to kill him and Harry had threatened to kill him all over again after old Sylvester had finished with him!

Sergeant Potts had taken Black Herbie to the scene of the theft in an effort to track down the bushranger. They had returned after many weary hours to report failure. The trail had been lost on ground so hard and rocky that not even the keen eyes of the black tracker could find it. The police were still searching, but as Potts told the squatter the bushranger was probably hundreds of miles away by now.

Old Sylvester had debated for a long time how adequately to punish his erring son and had then hit upon the method.

"You love horses and you love your home, George," he said. "If you are deprived of both for a time, it might teach you to be obedient in the future. School starts again in a week's time. I shall send you to your Aunt Bertha for a month, and if you as much as mount a horse during that time, you will stay there for six months. Regard yourself as serving a gaol sentence."

George had now been with his aunt for a fortnight, and had been at the town school for a week. He rather liked the school and the boy friends he had made, especially a humorous and tough lad named Eric Jones, whom everyone called "Jonah," Jack Grace and Harold Thorley. They were very friendly souls with whom he had chummed at once. Jonah, though tough, had a heart of gold. He was prime mover in all the school escapades. George even had a good word for the teacher, Mr. Herbert Hector, a long-suffering man who did his best to educate the wild bush material under his charge.

George smiled as he thought of the way Jonah, Jack, Harold and some of the other boys carried on in school. It was different to the small bush school he attended a few miles from his home.

As he ate his tea, his aunt looked at him fondly. She liked George, and thought him a well-behaved boy, but she quite approved of his father's action in sending him into exile for a month over the episode of Blackie.

George had been very downhearted when he had arrived at her home, but appeared now to be settling down. Actually, the only thing that hurt the lad was being deprived of his beloved Ginger. But there were only two more weeks to go.

"Enjoying yourself, George?" she asked.

"Yes, Auntie, but I do miss Ginger. Dad certainly knew how to punish me when he stopped me riding horses for a month."

An understanding soul, Aunt Bertha did not hurt the lad by telling him that it was all his own fault. Instead she asked, "How do you like the school here, George?"

"It is good and I have made some good friends, too," he replied. "That Eric Jones is a funny fellow. He makes everyone call him 'Jonah' because he says Eric is a sissy name. Do you know him, Aunt Bertha?"

"I know him all right and I think he is a first class larrikin," said Aunt Bertha severely. "He is always getting into trouble and mischief."

"He is, that," said George with a grin. "You don't know what he is going to do next."

"He'll end up in gaol, I know that," she answered.

Next day as they sat in school, George wondered what Jonah had up his sleeve in the way of mischief that day. He was watching Jonah who sat in front of him, when his attention was diverted to Mr. Hector, the teacher, who was rapping his cane smartly on the desk.

"English composition," remarked the teacher sternly, "is a subject in which this class is extremely backward."

He broke off and, for a few seconds, fixed Eric Jones with an unwavering stare which Jonah received between the eyes without even blinking.

"Of course," continued Mr. Hector, addressing the class generally, "there are certain pupils who are quite good at English but they are, I regret to say, in a minority. Other boys and girls are not only weak in composition but in grammar."

Jonah, who was not only weak in English composition and grammar but in history, arithmetic, geography, spelling, reading, writing and one or two other subjects, gave a disrespectful yawn like a very tired old cattle dog, but the rest of the class awaited the conclusion of the teacher's discourse with apprehension. Past experience had taught them that when old Hector talked as he was now doing, there was certain to be a most unpleasant sequel.

"The majority of you are no credit to me." said Mr. Hector sorrowfully. "I do my best, goodness knows, but who can drive sense into blocks of wood? But I will not give up. I am determined to persevere. I must and will discover if there is any talent hidden deep down inside you."

Once again he paused, and swept a stern eye over the class. The class favoured him with a united stare of consternation, sensing impending disaster.

"I am going to introduce a new subject to this class and that is the composition of poetry. Many people would say that in doing this I am just daring fate and courting certain disaster; and why would they say that?"

The teacher paused and looked at the class. His eye chanced to rest for a moment upon the strained visage of Jack Grace, who wriggled like a wounded snake, but felt called upon to say something.

"I dunno, sir," he muttered.

"You surprise me, Grace, really you do," said Mr. Hector. "Well, I shall tell you. People would be surprised at my suggesting that I should ask this class to compose poetry when its members cannot even spell properly and their efforts at ordinary composition would make the angels weep. Perhaps I am foolish."

"Yes, sir," said Jack Grace.

Mr. Hector looked at him and was on the point of saying something. Instead, he just sighed.

"As I said before," he went on, "I am determined to find out if there is any hidden talent among my pupils. Who knows but there may be a worthy successor to Shakespeare among you children?"

His sarcasm was quite lost upon the class. In fact one or two of the pupils preened themselves slightly. The majority, however, looked definitely scared. They were not poets and they knew it.

"Each of you, therefore," concluded Mr. Hector, "will bring me tomorrow at least four lines of original poetry. And see that you do so."

The class gasped with united consternation and one small girl began to cry. Jonah contented himself with making a noise like a wounded sheep caught in a barbed wire fence.

"A bloke like Hector," he said to Jack Grace, George Sylvester and Harold Thorley as they wended their way homewards after school, "ought to have his big toe shoved through a chaff-cutter." The rest of the boys agreed heartily.

"A man," added Jonah viciously, "ought to go and poison all his chooks." Again the boys agreed heartily.

"I'll think that over," said Jonah darkly. "I'll poison the lot of them."

"Good on you, Jonah," said Jack cordially. "Do it tonight."

"Can't," said Jonah bitterly. "I've got to stay home and write silly poetry."

"Gosh, yes," said the others gloomily.

"Ah, well, I feel a bit sorry for you blokes," said Archie Farrell, known to the boys as "Fido," who had joined them. "I'll be set. I'm a bit of a dabster at poetry. How does this sound? I made it up a few minutes ago. Seemed to come to me out of the sky, you know."

"Oh, chop out the bragging, Fido," grunted Jonah. "I can't put up with your silliness right now. I've got things on my mind. But if you've got poetry already written, get it off your chest and then beat it before I flatten your nose."

"Wash out your ears, then, and listen," said Fido inelegantly. "Here goes...

"Me and Jonah are good mates,
When we go to school we ain't never late,
Old Hector is a silly old coot,
And Jonah ought to give him a good hard boot."

"Why, you silly looking fool," shouted Jonah. "If you go writing that and showing it to Hector tomorrow, you'll be the clever joker who will get a good, hard boot, and don't you forget it."

Fido looked scornful.

"I ain't gonna write that out for Hector," he said. "He'll get something a lot better than that. I just gave you that sample to show you what I could do."

"It's the silliest rubbish I've ever heard," said Jack Grace.

"Do better," sneered Fido.

"Well, what about this: *A violet by a mossy stone, halfhidden from the eye fair as a star when only one is shining in the sky,"* said Jack in one breath.

"Hey, Jack, that's good!" said Jonah admiringly. "Make up another bit, go on!"

"Just a minute, Jonah," began Fido Farrell.

"Shut up, Fido," commanded Jonah. "Give Jack a fair go."

Jack thought hard for a moment and then,

"It's of a wild Colonial boy, Jack Dowling was his name of poor but honest parents he was born in Castlemaine he was his father's only son his mother's pride and joy and dearly did they always love their wild Colonial boy..."

Jack got that far in one breath-taking torrent of words when he was interrupted by a frantic Fido Farrell.

"Hey, hold your horses a minute," he exclaimed. "You didn't make up that bit of poetry. I know it myself. It's all about a bushranger bloke. Everybody knows that song."

"That ain't a fact," roared Jack.

"It is a fact!" shouted Fido.

"Take no notice of that jealous coot, Jack," said Jonah. "Just because he ain't as good as you, he is only getting jealous."

"I tell you…" bellowed Fido excitedly.

"Ease off, Fido, or you'll get a punch in the eye," said Jonah coldly. "If there's one bloke I don't like it is a bloke who gets jealous when another bloke does something better than he can."

"But, Jonah…"

"Ease off, I tell you!"

And Fido, muttering dark things, decided to "ease off."

Jonah bent a respectful eye upon Jack and asked him to continue. Jack, however, refused. He said that his efforts were not appreciated by certain persons present and he preferred not to continue.

"Well, what about you, Stinker?" said Jonah, glaring at Harold Thorley.

"Yes, I think I could make up a few lines if Fido Farrell will permit me," said Harold with dignity.

"If he opens his big mouth and says anything, I'll punch him on it and break six of his teeth," promised Jonah and, with this assurance, Harold, after a thoughtful pause, remarked:

"There is not in this wide world a valley so sweet
As that vale in whose bosom the bright waters meet;
Oh, the last rays …."

"You can punch me if you like, Jonah," screamed Fido, "but Stinker ain't gonna get away with that. Why, stone the crows, that's a song my sister's got at home on the piano."

Jonah heaved a great sigh and doubled a fist.

"I warned you, Fido, to keep that big mouth of yours shut," he said. "You wouldn't listen, you jealous coot, so take this to go on with…"

Saying which, Jonah administered a hearty punch to the

base of Fido Farrell's right ear. Fido howled in agony, while Jack Grace looked sadly at Harold Thorley.

"That was a rough one to put over on your mates, Stinker," he said.

"What?" asked Jonah.

"Me and you and old Stinkpot are all good mates, so I guess you won't mind me pointing out that what Harold just recited is really a song wrote by a feller named Tom Moore."

"Who, the barber over at Eastville?" asked Jonah with interest.

"Couldn't say," replied Jack. "Some bird named Tom Moore, anyway."

"But that barber bloke is half-silly," said Jonah. "He couldn't make up a song."

"All poets are silly," said Jack profoundly.

"That's true enough," replied Jonah.

"Jack Grace is a liar," said Harold Thorley. "That was my own poem."

Jonah shook his head. He looked distressed.

"If old Jack says Tom Moore the barber wrote it, then Tom Moore the barber wrote it," he said. "I'm surprised at you, Harold."

"Wot about my ear?" yelled Fido Farrell.

"I owed you that one," said Jonah tersely.

"Yes, and why don't you give Jack and Stinker a crack too?" said Fido. "They both said bits of poetry they didn't write. It's all right for Jack to say things about Stinker, but he is as bad himself."

"Hop it, Fido," instructed Jonah. "Don't go running my mates down. Stinker was just joking. He wouldn't do it on purpose. He is an honest feller like me. I'd cut my throat before I would steal a bit of poetry from a book and call it my own."

Fido opened his mouth to say something, but did not like the look on Jonah's face. He therefore closed it again and departed.

At school next morning there were many strained looks,

but Mr. Hector got off the mark at once. He informed the class that each pupil was to read out his or her effort when his or her name was called and then he would collect all the efforts and go through them carefully.

"They may need a little polishing up," he said sarcastically. "Perhaps a little touch here and there before they are submitted to the publisher to be issued in book form."

The class merely gaped at him.

"Attention, please!" rapped out Hector. "Johnson, you have the honour to be first."

Caught off balance, Teddy Johnson, a look in his eye like a stricken fly that sees the spider bearing down upon it, lurched to his feet, coughed softly like a horse with a touch of bronchitis, pulled from his pocket an exceedingly dirty piece of paper, and began:

> *"Old Mother Beck had a rope round her neck,*
> *Her arm in a sling and her eye knocked in,*
> *But she sat upon the floor with a lolly in her jaw*
> *Singing God Save the King."*

The class howled with delight, but Mr. Hector did not seem to be amused.

"Wretched boy!" he said to the hapless Teddy. "Your so-called poetry is both coarse and disgusting. Come out here!"

Teddy wandered out in front of the class to receive his reward—three resounding cuts with the cane. He wandered back to his seat with the palms of his hands tucked under his armpits and a look of agony upon his face.

Having restored order, Mr. Hector invited Barney Owens to oblige with his own, unaided effort. Barney obliged:

> *"A little bird squatted in a tree,*
> *A pretty little bird was he;*
> *A nasty little boy who had a catapult in his right hand*
> *Fired a brick at the little bird which crashed into the sand."*

"Rather morbid, Owens," remarked Mr. Hector.

"He couldn't do it," said Jonah.

"Talking in class, Jones," said Hector sternly. "Who couldn't do what?"

"He couldn't fire a brick out of a shanghai with his right hand. He would have to use both hands," Jonah pointed out. "How would he hold the stone in the pouch of the shanghai? With his mouth, huh?"

"He held it in his left hand, Jonah," exclaimed Barney. "You don't expect me to shove everything into the poem, do you? Ain't you got no commonsense at all?"

"I sometimes doubt whether Jones has got any commonsense, but that doesn't excuse you from talking in class, Owens. Kindly keep silent. You too, Jones. Nobody is interested in how shanghais or catapults are fired."

"I am," said Jonah.

"Silence!" roared Mr. Hector. "Another remark from you, Jones, and you'll get six cuts with the cane and will stay in after school for an hour."

"Yes, sir." said Jonah meekly.

"Thorley is the next boy to show what he can do and I trust that his effort will be a little superior to Owens's," said Hector.

Harold stood up and smirked. Then:

> *"There was a little man and he had a little gun*
> *And his bullets were made of lead, lead, lead;*
> *He went to the brook and found a little duck*
> *And he shot it right through the head, head, head"*

"Pup—please, Mister Hector, I've heard that before," claimed a small girl on the feminine side of the class.

Mr. Hector nodded grimly.

"We shall attend to Thorley later," he said darkly.

"Please, sir..." began Harold fearfully.

"Keep quiet, Thorley," ordered the teacher.

Even Jonah was familiar with the tragedy of the duck at the brook and mentally he endorsed Mr. Hector's action in telling Harold to keep quiet.

"Parsons, you are next," said the teacher. Syd Parsons, looking unhappy, was ready:

"I saw a dead goat lying in the midst of a paddock.
So I wrapped him up in my father's new Sunday coat,
Then I rowed across the river in my boat,
And buried the dead goat with my old kangaroo dog."

Mr. Hector looked rather pained at this.

"While congratulating you upon your most humane behaviour, Parsons," he said, "I'm afraid that as a poetical effort, your lines are..." He broke off and mused silently.

"Pup-please, sir," piped up the interfering small girl again, "Catface Parsons ain't never had a kangaroo dog in his life. He ain't got a boat either. He don't live anywhere near the river."

"His old man ain't had a new Sunday coat for donkey's years," added Jonah.

"Apparently neither Mr. Jones nor Miss Field have heard of poetic licence," said Mr. Hector. "Have you?"

"No, sir," replied Mr. Jones and Miss Field together.

"Then do not presume to criticise and do not presume to set yourselves up as authorities upon a subject of which you both are bottomless wells of ignorance," Mr. Hector said. That silenced both Mr. Jones and Miss Field for quite a few minutes.

In the meantime, the poems were being delivered one by one. As they progressed, so did the gloom of Mr. Hector deepen. In his class he could not see another Henry Lawson or Lord Macauley.

When it came to Jack Grace's turn, Jonah sat up expectantly. This, he told himself, would be good—a gem of Australian verse destined to go down in literary history.

"I have a little pony which I ride to school each day,
But when I ain't riding him my father shoves him in the hay cart.
My little pony bucked me off,
I fell into the hay one day,
And when me old man came along,
He said don't cry Jack, and I'll sing you a nice song."

"Help!" exclaimed Jonah. "Fancy Jack's old man singing a nice song."

"Talking again, Jones!" rapped out Mr. Hector.

"Was just saying that Jack's father can't sing songs for nuts," said Jonah meekly.

"It is to be hoped that he is a better singer than his son is a poet," replied the teacher.

"Please, sir," said Jonah, "I don't think Jack was right in saying that he rode a pony to school every day and that he uses it in the hay cart. Jack walks to school and a pony is too little to pull a hay cart along."

"Poetic licence, Jones," said Hector.

"Oh, that again," said Jonah and lapsed into immediate silence. Mr. Hector looked at him.

"Jones," he said, "I think it is time that the class was favoured with your own effort. You have been rather forward in criticising the work of your fellow pupils. Let us now hear from you."

"Certainly, sir," said Jonah with alacrity and sprang to his feet, at the same time hauling a sheet of grubby paper from his trouser pocket.

"Listen to this, sir," he invited.

"Oft when the camps were dreaming,
And stars began to pale,
Through rugged ranges gleaming,
Swept on the Royal Mail.
Behind five foaming horses,
And lit by flashing lamps,
Old Cobb and Co. in royal state
Went dashing past the camps."

Here Jonah paused to get his wind back. The class gazed at him in wonder mixed with awe; Mr. Hector looked stunned and on the point of fainting. Jonah noted with pleasure the effect his oration had had, and continued:

> *"I hear the fall of timber.*
> *From distant flats and fells..."*

"Jones," bellowed Hector, regaining consciousness. "Stop! You hear the fall of timber do you? You will shortly feel the fall of a cane! SIT DOWN!"

Jonah looked surprised, but sat down, nevertheless. Mr. Hector pulled himself together.

"I will be calm," he said, and paused for a few seconds to attain that desirable state of mind. Then:

"Boys and girls," he said. "We are honoured today. But one moment." He paused and bent upon Jonah a ferocious eye— the type of eye with which a hungry tiger might glance at a fat antelope innocently drinking at a sylvan stream.

"Come out here, Jones," he roared. "And do not stand too close to me or I may do something to you that I will regret."

Jonah lurched to his feet, went out and stood facing the class.

"Children," said the teacher with deadly calm. "Kindly permit me to present to you one of the greatest Australian poets of all time. Meet Mr. Henry Lawson. Until today I have never believed in miracles."

The class did not understand. It merely blinked at the master and sat like a collection of stuffed mullets. Harold Thorley, already booked for the cane, moaned like a wounded terrier. He had been hoping to get off lightly, but with Mr. Hector in his present frame of mind, anything was likely to occur.

This thought made him moan again. Mr. Hector heard the sad noise and looked at him.

"You had better come out here too, Thorley," he said, and

Harold obeyed him. He lined up at Jonah's side and looked scared.

"We will first finish the poetical recital and then we shall deal with this pair," said Mr. Hector. "Farrell is the next."

Fido Farrell rose to his feet and burbled.

"Please Mister Hector, sir, I never wrote nothing. I didn't have time last night," he whined as he tried to hide a piece of paper behind his back.

"What is that paper in your hand?"

"Paper, sir?"

"Yes, paper. Let me see it."

"Ain't nothing, sir."

"Read what is on that paper, Farrell, and be quick about it," snapped Mr. Hector. "I am in no mood for funny business."

"Read it for the love of Pete, Fido," begged Jonah.

Mr. Hector ignored Jonah. He was intent upon Fido, who slowly and reluctantly withdrew his hand from behind his back, smoothed out the paper and began:—

"Attend all ye who list to hear our noble England's praise,
I tell of the thrice famous deeds she wrought in ancient days.
When that great fleet invincible…"

Fido just could not go on. He broke down and looked at Hector. The light in that tortured man's eyes was a danger signal nobody could mistake.

"Farrell," he shrieked, "out you come!" Fido joined Harold and Jonah and the trio waited for the skies to fall.

"I am not going to comment on Thorley's efforts in words," said Mr. Hector. "I shall cane him for his exhibition." He did so. Six of the best. Harold returned to his seat and wished he were dead.

"Now, boys and girls," said Mr. Hector. "It is my duty to introduce you to Lord Macauley. Henry Lawson you already know. To me this will always be a red-letter day—the occasion upon which I caned, and caned severely, two of the world's greatest poets."

Jonah looked at Fido. Fido looked at Jonah. Then they both looked at Mr. Hector. The class drank in the trio. During the next few seconds the air was filled with the sound of a swishing cane.

After school Teddy Johnson came up to Jonah wearing a smirk on his visage.

"Say, Jonah," he said cheerfully to that well-caned and over-wrought lad, "I spent a lot of time making up this poem. It wasn't taken out of a book, either. What d'you think of it?"

"During the week we will hear many howls,
From Jonah and Fido, the two silly fowls;
For they both did a thing that we all know is crook—
They pinched some poems from out of a book."

Teddy grinned when he had finished and asked Jonah how he liked the thing. Jonah breathed deeply like an angry bull and turned to Farrell.

"Ready, Fido?" he asked.

"Ready, Jonah," said Fido.

They both fell upon Teddy Johnson. Both had their pent-up feelings to relieve and they relieved them upon the person of Teddy Johnson. When it was over, Teddy had two black eyes and a number of other minor injuries.

Then, taking Fido by the arm and with a look of peace upon his face, Jonah turned his head towards the setting sun, and spoke:

"Shifto, Fido?"

"Shifto, Jonah."

Arm in arm they departed into the gathering dusk home-wards—Henry Lawson and Lord Macauley.

George Sylvester, choking with laughter, followed them. He told himself that he was going to invite Jonah to spend a week-end at the Sylvester station with him when he returned home. He felt certain that wherever Jonah might be there would be a lot of fun.

CHAPTER VII.

BLACKIE THE BUSHRANGER

AFTER Johnny Gibson left young George Sylvester standing at the side of the bush track, he rode through the dense scrub for about two miles and then pulled up. Dismounting, he approached Blackie and stroked his arched satin neck. The black stallion, who always responded readily to kindness, nickered softly and rubbed his head up and down the bushranger's sleeve.

"Feeling pally, eh?" asked Gibson. "That's fine. Whoever broke you in knew his job all right. It is hard to believe that you were born and bred a brumby. Now, let me see if you are just as pally with me in the saddle."

Gibson placed his foot in the stirrup and swung himself into the saddle. Blackie received the burden quietly. He had nothing against this man, though he did wonder a little what had become of young George.

"I'll ride you back to the camp to get you used to me," the bushranger told him. Blackie twitched his ears, but went forward willingly enough when Gibson urged him. Soon he was trotting freely, Gibson leading his own horse by its reins.

"What a stroke of luck, getting him with no trouble at all," the bushranger mused as he rode along.

Johnny Gibson and Bert Wall, plying their unlawful trade many miles away, had heard of this magnificent horse on the Sylvester property, and as good horses meant everything to them—their liberty, perhaps their very lives—they had set out to steal him. Unknown in these parts, Gibson had proposed that he visit the Sylvester station on the pretence of seeking a job. While there he would have a look at Blackie and judge if all the reports he had heard of the black horse were true. If they were, he would spy out the land and make plans to steal the horse one night. Fortunately for him, if not for Harry Hornsby and George, he did not have to carry out the plan. The lad's disobedience had delivered the wanted animal into his hands with a minimum of trouble.

And Blackie appeared to live up to all the reports of him.

Gibson grinned as he rode along. He was making for a camp that he and Bert Wall had established in the hills—a secure hideout for men of their kind. The type of country, wild and rocky, was ideally suitable, in that it would defy the best black tracker in the world to trace them.

Nearing the camp, he gave a low whistle, which was instantly acknowledged with another, and Bert Wall emerged from the scrub. He was a desperate-looking character, badly in need of a haircut and a shave. He looked surprised when he saw his mate with two horses.

"Where did you pick up that beauty, Johnny?" he asked.

"This is Blackie the brumby," said Gibson proudly. "Got him already."

"How in the name of fortune did you manage that so soon?"

Gibson dismounted and led the two horses through the trees and brush to the clearing where a rough bark shanty had been thrown together. He tied them both to trees near Wall's own horse. Blackie did not appreciate this. He did not like the company and after he had shown it by attempting to kick Wall's mount, Gibson untied him and led him to another tree.

When Gibson had told his mate the story, Wall looked thoughtful.

"I think you made a mistake telling that kid who you were, Johnny," he said slowly. "He'll put the police on us as sure as the Murrumbidgee is a river."

"Let him," said Gibson. "It will take more than the traps on their useless nags to catch up with us. We'll move tonight."

"Suit me," said Wall briefly. "I'm sick of this place."

The two bushrangers rode most of that night, and when dawn's first light was in the sky, arrived at a small settlement where they had secret friends. Here they left Gibson's spare horse and young George's saddle and bridle and, after a meal and a short rest, rode off again to parts far distant.

And though the police and black trackers searched high and low for the pair, they did not succeed in catching up with them. Their camp in the hills was discovered, but the tracks were too old to follow. Nothing was heard of Gibson and Wall for weeks and then an outbreak of robberies, far away from the Sylvester station, showed that the pair were up to their old tricks again...

Stories came through to the police of coaches bailed up and passengers robbed, lone swagmen taken down for the few pounds they possessed, wayside inns and homesteads ransacked, stations rifled, Chinese gold diggers deprived of everything they had, and many other incidents. Stories were told too, of the magnificent black horse ridden by one of the bushrangers. This horse was as fast as the wind, and nothing could catch him. In one daring daylight raid on a station, the outlaws had stolen a famous racing mare, leaving another horse in her place.

Police troopers and revengeful property owners who set out to hunt the robbers always returned empty handed. On several occasions the bushrangers had deliberately lingered at the scene of a crime apparently to give the police the chance to chase them. The police accepted the various challenges; but their horses were snails compared with Gibson on Blackie and Wall on the racing mare.

Old John Sylvester, reading these reports in the newspapers, was guilty of using quite a lot of bad language.

"There's that Blackie for you," he said loudly to Hornsby. "He is as big an outlaw as Gibson and Wall. Didn't I tell you he had bad blood in him?"

"I don't know about that, boss," protested Hornsby. "I think you said he had good blood. Anyway, remember his mother was a thoroughbred."

"And his father was a dashed bushranging brumby like he is himself," growled the old man. "Where the dickens is that young George? I'll..."

But George wasn't there. He had sneaked silently away. He knew he was to blame for the theft of Blackie, but he was fed up to the eyebrows with having the fact continually rubbed into him. He had been home some time from his exile in the big town, and had been allowed to resume riding Ginger.

George's new friend. Eric Jones, was due to visit the station that week-end, and the lad hoped and prayed that Wall and Gibson would take a holiday from thieving for a while so that the atmosphere would quieten, otherwise Jonah might not have the good time that had been planned for him. This included long horse rides, George on Ginger and Jonah on another horse George had selected for him. Jonah had boasted that he was quite an accomplished horseman, though George had never seen him ride.

The days passed without further news of Gibson and Wall, and when Friday night arrived, so did Eric Jones. He turned up at the station with his spare clothes in a sugar bag and a large grin on his freckled face. He told George that he had got a lift all the way in a buggy driven by an old settler who had been visiting the town.

"Saved the coach fare," he said. "Cobb and Co. will go broke."

"I'll leave you boys to yourselves," said Mr. Sylvester, after George had introduced Eric. "You look after Eric, George, and see that he enjoys himself."

"I'll do that all right, Dad," replied George, and took Jonah to his room.

"Listen, George," said the visitor as he up ended the sugar bag and cascaded a nightshirt and a few other odds and ends on the floor, "for the love of Mike, don't call me Eric. I don't like the name. It's sissy. Call me Jonah and tell your old man and all the rest of the mob here to do the same."

"All right, Eric," laughed George.

"I'll crown you if you call me that again!" snorted the guest. George laughed heartily. The presence of another lad in his home was a great joy to him.

"What will we do tomorrow?" asked Jonah. "Got anything up your sleeve except your arm?"

"I thought we might get out the horses and go for a long ride. We could take some tucker with us and have a picnic."

"That sounds fair enough," agreed Jonah. "What about guns? Could we do a bit of shooting, do you reckon?"

"I reckon," said George "I've got three rifles."

"Well, that's that fixed," said Jonah. "Hope you can lend me a good horse. I can ride all right, so don't go working off some tame old broken-down prad on me."

"I'm going to lend you Peter. He is as good as my own horse Ginger, and that's saying a lot."

"Right!" was the terse comment.

The two lads sat far into the night discussing their plans and when at last they decided to seek their beds, they were very tired but very happy.

CHAPTER VIII.

BLACKIE TURNS UP

AS soon as it was daylight, George was up and dressed. He went to Jonah's room and found that lad still asleep and snoring like a pig. Without wasting a word, he grabbed his guest by a foot that was sticking out from under the clothes and pulled him from the bed on to the floor with a bump.

Jonah gave a yell and began to struggle with the bedclothes, getting himself properly tangled up.

Incoherent with laughter, George extricated his breathless friend and told him to get a move on with his dressing. "I want you to have a look around the place before breakfast," he said.

"That's fine," said Jonah, and got dressed in record time. First stop was the stables, where George introduced Jonah to Ginger and Peter. The latter was a sturdy chestnut and Jonah instantly approved of him.

"Shove a saddle and bridle on him, George, and let me have a crack at him," said Jonah. George saddled and bridled Peter and led him from the stable. Jonah mounted like an expert and trotted the horse round the yard a few times. When he dismounted he expressed himself as being entirely satisfied with the horse.

They found Mr. Sylvester just finishing breakfast. He greeted them warmly and the meal was punctuated by cheery chatter.

"Have a good day out, lads," said the squatter as he left the table, and they both assured him that they would.

Half an hour later, with well filled saddle bags and their rifles slung over their shoulders, George and Jonah were on their way. George intended to visit old Fred the swagman for a brief talk before moving onwards, and told Jonah about the old man as they rode along.

"He's crazy on birds, Jonah," said George, "so don't say anything about shooting. If he sees us carrying rifles, say we are after rabbits and foxes."

When they reached the hut, old Fred was not in sight. The door was closed and no smoke came from the chimney.

"Looks as if he's bolted," remarked Jonah.

They both climbed off their horses and at George's suggestion unslung their rifles and stood them at the side of the hut. George then knocked on the old door.

"Come in, friend," he heard a faint voice say and, pushing the door wide, he saw, in the dim light, old Fred lying on his bunk.

"You're sleeping in late, Fred," said the boy.

"Come on in, George, and bring your friend," said the swagman. "I'm not feeling too well today."

George opened the window, which was merely pieces of bark nailed to a rude framework, and allowed the sun to stream into and light up the gloomy old hut.

"Meet a friend of mine, Fred. His name is Eric Jones," he said.

"Pleased to meet you, Eric," said the old man, extending his toil-worn hand.

"Don't call me Eric, call me Jonah," said the owner of that distinguished title as he took the swagman's hand.

George looked at old Fred closely.

"You don't look good, Fred," he said. "Been sick?"

"I'm afraid so. Getting old on it now, you know. Been lying

here now for a couple of days. Haven't been able to move around much. I wonder if you would do me a favour, lad?"

"Name it and it's done."

"Would you go to Jasper Spender's shanty and get me some tobacco? I've run out and I'm lost without baccy for my old pipe. I tried a bit of bark, but it's not the same."

"I should think not!" said George with a shudder, while Jonah grinned widely.

"I once tried tea leaves in a clay pipe and they made me as sick as a dog," he said reminiscently

"Hey? A young boy like you shouldn't go around smoking tea leaves!" said old Fred severely. "You cut that out."

"I have, I assure you, old feller," said Jonah.

"And tobacco too. You leave that alone;" said Fred.

Jonah grinned and said nothing.

"Jonah and I are going on a horse ride and picnic, but I'll ride over to Spender's store for you first, Fred," said George. "It won't take me more than ten minutes."

"Where is this here store?" demanded Jonah.

"It's along the road to the township and miles from anywhere," explained his friend. "A lonely place, but handy for travellers. He sells everything from a needle to an anchor."

"What does a bloke want with an anchor in the bush?" asked Jonah.

"Old Jasper could do with one to keep his prices down," said old Fred with a faint smile.

It was arranged that Jonah should stay with old Fred and do any little jobs for him, also get his breakfast and boil his billy. Jonah grabbed an old broom made of tea-tree branches and began to sweep the hut out, while George mounted Ginger and rode off whistling. He crossed a small bridge, struck the track that led to the main road and cantered along this to Spender's bush store. It was a large, sprawling old place and its owner was a wild looking old chap with a long beard and a shock of hair that looked as if it had never had the attention of a barber for many years.

Old Jasper greeted George suspiciously and in a surly manner.

"What do you want, young Sylvester?" he demanded. "Whatever it is, I haven't got it."

"Well, then," said George, who knew the old man's ways, "I'll have a shilling's worth wrapped up in brown paper."

"Cheek! Dashed cheek!" snapped Jasper. "How's your old man, anyway?"

"My respected father," said George with dignity, "is quite well, thank you."

"Come, come, what do you want? I can't stand here all day arguing the toss with young whipper-snappers."

"Tobacco," said George.

"You won't get it here. You're too young to smoke."

"It's for old Fred. He's too sick to come and get it himself."

"How sick is he? Ain't dead is he?" growled Jasper.

"No, but you will be if you try any tricks," came a sinister voice from the doorway. "Stick your hands up, Spender, and you, too, youngster!"

George and Jasper swung round and glared at the doorway. Framed in the opening was a man, a pistol in his hand, pointing straight at them!

"Johnny Gibson!" gasped young George.

"Ah, my little mate who gave me the brumby!" exclaimed the bushranger. "Thanks a lot, boy. He's done me proud!"

"What do you want, you robbing, thieving scoundrel?" roared Spender angrily.

"Don't be so insulting, Jasper," said Gibson reprovingly. "I merely want all the cash you've got in this barn, plus a swag of tucker."

"I'll see you dead first!"

"It won't be me who'll be dead if there is any funny business," said the bushranger darkly. "Get a move on. As for you, youngster, you keep still or you'll collect a bullet too."

"What have you done with Blackie?" asked George suddenly.

"He's outside, quite safe. By the way, do you own that other nag that was tied up to the hitching post?"

"That's my horse Ginger," said George. "What have you done to him?"

"Nothing. When I came along and saw him there, I thought it safer to release him in case his owner might take a fancy to chase me," said Gibson. "I took him into the bush, gave him a fright, and sent him home. Looks as if you'll have to walk back, son. When ever we meet it seems that you have to take a walk after."

"I didn't hear you outside," said George.

"I don't generally kick up a row when I'm doing things," said Gibson.

"I want Blackie!" shouted George. "You're a scoundrel, Johnny Gibson!"

"Stow that loud talk or I'll bash you down!" threatened the bushranger. "Not that there is anyone to hear you outside!"

But Gibson was wrong. Blackie, tied to the hitching post, had recognised the boy's voice. Into his mind flooded memories of a young human being who had been his friend and with whom he had spent pleasant hours. His life with the Gibson had been interesting and exciting and he had been treated well; but he had missed the pleasant association with the lad. He strained at the reins tied to the post, trying to get loose to have a look at his young friend.

"I'd like to see Blackie again," remarked George.

"Stay where you are," said Gibson. "After this old devil has given me what I want, you may have the pleasure of seeing me ride away on Blackie. That is the only glimpse you'll get of him. Now, Spender, get busy!"

Under the threat of the revolver, the storekeeper began to shove goods into a sugar bag, grunting and muttering as he did so. Gibson kept a strict eye on both him and George. His back was turned to the door and he did not notice the new arrival.

It was Blackie!

Gibson, in case he had to make a quick escape, had not tied the reins tightly to the post and when Blackie started to pull and strain, they came loose. The horse ambled to the door of the store and shoved an amiable nose inside, desiring to find out if his young friend was indeed there.

Though Gibson did not see Blackie, George did. Blackie nickered softly, but the bushranger, not knowing the horse was loose, took no notice.

"If only I could make a dash for it," the lad said to himself.

He dared not make a move. Gibson was watching him and if he ran for the door, the man could shoot him before he reached it. Even if he did succeed in mounting the horse, Gibson's revolver could drop him before he could ride three yards. It was agony for the boy but he had to endure it. The only bright spot was that Blackie obviously had been well looked after and appeared to be in the pink of condition.

The doorway was too low for the horse to enter the store. He was puzzled about George. He and the lad had always been friends, yet the boy was ignoring him. He was also being ignored by his other friend, Gibson, whose back was towards him. It was all very perplexing.

Blackie nickered his disappointment. Gibson took no notice, but this time Spender, moving around behind the slab counter, glanced at the doorway and saw the horse. He opened his mouth to say something, caught a look in George's eyes, and closed it again. George's glance said quite plainly, "Say nothing about the horse."

"Mr. Gibson," said George, "is Blackie very fast?"

"The fastest in the country," said the bushranger proudly.

"If I was on his back now," said the lad, his eye now on Spender, "I'd ride like wildfire for the police."

"Haw, haw, haw!" roared Gibson. "I bet you would, you young villain!"

Jasper Spender read the message in George's statement. He placed a good stock of groceries in the sugar bag and asked the outlaw if it was enough. Gibson nodded.

"I'll add a tin of my special blackberry jam, Gibson, and I hope it poisons you," said Jasper, and as the bushranger laughed, the storekeeper dived beneath the counter and appeared with a heavy tin.

"Here it is!" he bellowed and before Gibson could duck, the tin sailed through the air and hit him on the forehead.

As soon as the tin left Spender's hand, George went flying for the doorway. Blackie welcomed him with a glad whinny, but the lad wasted no time in greetings. He grabbed the reins, threw himself into the saddle, jerked the stallion's head round, and sent him flying down the road at a gallop. Blackie, overjoyed to have his young friend with him again, gave a loud neigh, and went like a streamlined tornado.

His heart in his mouth, and in expectation of bullets whizzing past his head, George crouched low over Blackie's mane and rode as he had never ridden before.

Back in the store, old Jasper Spender was sitting astride the fallen bushranger and was engaged in the exhilarating pastime of banging his head on the earthen floor. The heavy tin of jam had knocked Gibson flying and as he hit the ground, the storekeeper was on him. Gibson was unconscious when Jasper had finished with him, and then the storekeeper proceeded to tie him up with so much rope that the outlaw was almost invisible.

"That should hold him until that youngster returns with the troopers," said Jasper, looking down with satisfaction at the bound man.

George pulled up outside the police station and shouted loudly for Sergeant Potts. That officer came out and demanded to know what the excitement was about. George told him. Galvanised into action, the sergeant threw himself on his horse and together they set off at a fast gallop for Spender's store. As they neared it, they noticed a horse standing outside.

"Wonder what that means?" shouted Potts.

At that moment, two men ran from the store. They were Wall and Gibson. Spurring his horse hard, Potts rode down on them, loudly calling out to them to surrender.

"The traps!" exclaimed Wall and, raising a pistol, fired point blank at the charging sergeant. The bullet struck the police horse in the chest and the brave animal, with a loud scream of pain, crashed to earth, throwing his rider over his head. Wall quickly mounted his own horse and Gibson sprang up beside him. In a matter of seconds they were flying down the road in a cloud of dust.

As George flung himself from Blackie's back, Sergeant Potts rose from the ground, unhurt except for a few scratches. His uniform was covered in dust, but he did not care about that. A bruise on his cheek showed where his carbine had come into sharp contact with it as he hit the hard earth. The weapon itself was not damaged.

George took one look at the sergeant's dead horse.

"Mr. Potts," he said quickly, "here, you ride Blackie! He'll overtake those two scoundrels for you. He could catch anything, and as their horse is carrying a double load, they can't get away."

"The very thing, George! You have a look in the store and

see if those murdering devils have done anything to old Jasper. Get help for him if necessary, and also send a message to the police station for Trooper Sinclair to follow me."

"Yes, sergeant," replied the boy, and Potts tried to mount Blackie. That spirited steed, however, had other ideas. He resented the change of riders and let the sergeant know it. Potts managed to get into the saddle and then almost hit the ground again as Blackie reared and bucked.

George, who was making for the store, turned at the sergeant's shout and went running back. Blackie was giving a fine exhibition of buckjumping, and though the sergeant was an accomplished rider, he undoubtedly would have been unseated had not George taken a hand.

"Calm down, you villain!" he roared. "Behave yourself!"

He made a grab at the reins and was nearly jerked off his feet as Blackie reared and plunged wildly.

"Calm down!" George shouted. "Stop it Blackie, will you!"

Blackie heard him and, to the surprise and relief of the sergeant, did calm down. George patted the stallion's glossy neck and spoke to him soothingly. Blackie subsided and was good.

"Dash it, think of the time we're wasting," exclaimed the impatient Potts. "Those villains will be in Melbourne by now!"

He mounted, this time without any trouble, and Blackie, under his urging, flew down the road like a black arrow. George watched for a few seconds and then rushed to the store. When he entered, he could see no sign of the storekeeper until a low groan from behind the rough counter sent him there. Lying on the floor was Jasper Spender and he had blood on his face. Also, he appeared to be unconscious.

George forced his way behind the narrow counter and dropped to his knees.

"Are you all right, Mr. Spender?" he asked urgently. The

wounded man stirred and opened his eyes. He blinked at George and then rubbed his forehead with a trembling hand.

"What's going on?" he asked, feebly and gave another groan.

"Gibson and Wall, the bushrangers, were here. Don't you remember? What happened? Did they shoot you?"

"Give me a drink of water, youngster," gasped the storekeeper. George rushed to the rear of the store and hastily filled an old tin mug from an iron tank. When he returned, Spender was sitting up and looking around dazedly. He took the mug of water and gulped it down. George helped him to his feet and led him to an old wooden bench in the corner.

"I'll be all right, youngster," said the storekeeper. "That Wall fired a pistol at me, but it just creased my forehead. I fell down, meaning to play possum, but I must have bumped my head on something, because I was knocked out."

"But what happened after I left?" asked George.

Old Jasper explained that not very long after George's rapid exit to get the police, Bert Wall had arrived.

"I had my back to the door and was watching Gibson roped up on the floor," he went on. "Wall sneaked in and dug a gun into my back. He then made me untie Gibson, who was coming round. Gibson told him what had happened and that villain Wall fired at me. I dropped, and that's all I know. When I came round I found you here."

George told him what had happened since he had ridden away on Blackie and added, "They must have heard the sergeant and me coming, and got a scare."

"It looks like that. Well, I'm feeling not too bad now, George, but I think I'll close up the store for the rest of the day and have a lie down on my bunk."

George thought for a moment.

"If you are all right, Mr. Spender," he said, "I'd better see about getting help to Sergeant Potts. He is on his own and those two bushrangers are pretty desperate men."

"It's a long way to town, my lad. You can ride old Biddy if you like," said Spender doubtfully.

Biddy was the storekeeper's rather ancient mare that had seen many better days, but George was grateful for the offer.

Having made the storekeeper comfortable on his bunk, George locked up the store for him and then hurried round the back to the ramshackle shed in which Biddy lived. She eyed him sleepily and yawned mightily when he threw an ancient saddle, a perfect match for the old mare, on to her back, and fitted her with a bridle made chiefly of rope and string. Old Jasper had plenty of money but he did not live up to his surname.

When George climbed into the saddle, he could not persuade Biddy to indulge in anything faster than a shambling trot.

"This will never do," said the boy aloud. "It will be midnight before I get to town on this old crock. I wish I knew where Ginger was."

Struck by a sudden idea, he wheeled Biddy into the bush and headed for old Fred's hut. It took him nearly twenty minutes to reach it and when he did, he rushed inside and panted out his news to Jonah and the swagman.

"I want Peter," he said. "I'll never get anywhere with that piece of crows' food outside!"

"Hey, where do I come in?" shouted Jonah indignantly.

"You don't come in at all unless you like to ride Biddy. I've got to get a move on. See you later," said George. He grabbed his rifle, which was still leaning against the side of the hut, sprang into the saddle and rode as fast as Peter would take him towards town and the police station.

Jonah was almost weeping with disappointment and old Fred sympathised with him.

"I don't own a horse, or I'd lend you one," said the swagman. "Anyway, stay here where you are safe. You get hurt hunting bushrangers and police troopers."

"Get hurt, my grandmother's number sixteen foot!" roared Jonah ineloquently and indignantly. "Listen, Fred, how do you get to Spender's store? I'll ride that old Biddy crock there and wait for George and the trooper. They might give me a lift."

"And pigs might fly," grunted old Fred as he gave Jonah the necessary directions. Swinging his rifle across his back, he climbed on to old Biddy and flogged and kicked her into quite a respectable trot. He had no trouble locating the road and eventually the store. When he got there, he tried to rein in old Biddy outside the front door, but that obstinate animal proceeded round the back and came to a halt at the shed. Plainly, she had had enough of these goings on and wanted to call it a day. Jonah took off the saddle and bridle in disgust, threw them on the floor and returned on foot to the front of the store. What to do next was a problem. He spent a few minutes examining Sergeant Potts's dead horse, still lying on the road, but could get no inspiration from it. The police horse, beyond any shadow of doubt, was dead.

Sitting on the store doorstep and glooming to himself, Jonah was surprised to hear a horse whinny. He looked up and saw Ginger. That steed, having cantered off into the bush after Gibson had released him, had returned to look for his young master.

With a whoop of delight, Jonah grabbed the horse and mounted. Hitching his rifle comfortably over his shoulder, he set off up the road in the direction Sergeant Potts had taken.

CHAPTER IX.
THE END OF THE TRACK

AS he galloped along, Sergeant Potts cursed the bad luck that had caused the delay at the store when his own horse was shot front under him and when Blackie had played up. The brumby was now making up for it, but the delay might enable the bushrangers to get clean away. They had a good five minutes start on him and though he was travelling like the wind, he could not catch a glimpse of them ahead, nor even of dust that might betray their flight.

It was quite possible, the sergeant mused, that the outlaws had turned off into the bush, though the country here was very rough, especially for a horse carrying a double burden. In other circumstances he would have enjoyed the ride. Blackie moved like a graceful machine. The sergeant could feel the intense power of the stallion as his stride lengthened and he kept to his gait with the tirelessness of a bush-bred horse.

Potts watched the road speed towards him. Mile after mile passed under the flying hoofs, mile after mile of road that was merely an avenue through dense bush. He kept a close watch on the sides of the road as well as ahead. He could not be certain that the bushrangers would not hide at some vantage spot and shoot him from ambush.

Rounding a sharp bend, he was almost thrown from the saddle when Blackie shied suddenly and sidestepped to a nervous halt. Sitting with his back to a rock which jutted slightly into the road was a man with a swag at his feet. He looked at Potts and Potts looked at him.

"Funny place to have a rest," exclaimed the sergeant. "It's a wonder my horse didn't knock you down. What do you mean, hiding round corners, anyway?"

"I've been robbed," replied the man, who had a scraggy red beard and a terrified look in his eye.

"Who'd want to rob you?" snorted the sergeant.

"The two wild fellers on the one horse who came by about ten minutes ago," said the wayfarer, still sitting there. "I was walking along the track with me swag and they bailed me up. They took all me money, which wasn't much, only thirty bob, and told me to sit down and stay here for half an hour or they'd shoot me dead."

Sergeant Potts looked at the swagman closely, wondering if the wayfarer was trying to pull his leg. The man, however, appeared to be quite genuine, and not a little scared.

"Do you mean to tell me that you are going to do what they said?" demanded the police officer. "They'll be miles away by now. They know I'm on their track and they certainly won't come this way again."

"I don't want any trouble," replied the wayfarer obstinately.

"You're mad!" exclaimed the irritated sergeant.

"Maybe, and maybe not. I'm not mad enough to risk getting a bullet in me, anyhow."

"Which way did they go?"

"I'm not telling. They said I wasn't to say anything."

"Well, you'll tell me, my fine fellow, or I'll arrest you. You said you didn't want any trouble, didn't you?"

"I said that."

"Well, speak up, man, or you'll find yourself in trouble with the police," said Potts grimly.

"H'm, that's different," said the wayfarer after considering the point. "They rode off down that track over there between the two ironbarks. It leads down into a gully, I think, though I've never been there."

"All right. Now up on your feet and get a move on."

"I'm staying here until the half hour is up."

"Got a watch?"

"No."

"Well, how are you going to tell the time?"

"By the sun, sergeant, by the sun, as I have done, man and boy, for thirty years!" responded the swagman simply.

With an exclamation of disgust, Potts headed Blackie to the spot indicated by the wayfarer and found a well defined track. Dismounting, and leading Blackie by the reins, the sergeant proceeded cautiously along this track, which began to incline, winding downwards through the scrub until eventually it levelled out into a gully.

Leading Blackie with one hand and holding his service pistol in the other, Potts proceeded with the utmost caution. He did not know who or what he might meet. It was a difficult situation. He was alone, and though he was armed with rifle and revolver, he had to face two desperate men, also armed and ready to use those arms to avoid arrest. He calculated that it would be possibly two hours before he could expect any assistance.

George might not find any troopers at the police station and if he did, how could the party locate him and Blackie? The fool of a sundowner sitting at the rock might take it into his head to go in a direction opposite to the town. Reaching fairly open ground, Potts remounted and proceeded at a walking pace. He covered half a mile and then, in the distance, caught sight of a slight smoke haze. A camp fire!

The sergeant now exercised the greatest care. His revolver

gripped firmly, he drew nearer, and discovered a small clearing. Seated at a fire on which a billy can was boiling, were two men who had their backs towards him, but he knew them for Wall and Gibson. He wondered at their lack of caution, but realised that they had only to turn their heads and they would discover him. There was precious little cover for him to hide behind. Potts decided to take direct action. About two hundred yards separated him from the outlaws. Spurring Blackie into a smart canter, the gallant sergeant dashed straight at the camp fire, and with levelled pistol, shouted... "Surrender!"

Gibson and Wall sprang to their feet and turned round. Wall made a grab at the gun in his belt, but a shot from the sergeant's pistol hit the ground at his feet and he hurriedly put up his hands. So did Gibson.

"Throw your guns into the bushes and be quick about it!" ordered Potts and, with glares of hatred both men obeyed.

"You've got us sergeant, but what are you going to do with us?" asked Wall with a surly smile. "You're going to have a hard job getting us out of this place and into that lock-up."

"My men will be along in a few moments," said the sergeant with an assurance he did not feel.

"Tell that to the Governor of Fiji," scoffed Gibson.

"You're on your own, Potts." Keeping a wary eye on the pair, the sergeant dismounted and stood at Blackie's head. The horse whinnied and Gibson looked at it.

"Hullo there, Blackie, how's tricks?" he called out, and the black stallion nickered a greeting.

"Old mates, aren't we, Blackie?" asked the bushranger, and grinned as Blackie stretched out his neck and snorted. Blackie knew Gibson, of course. They had had a lot of good, though strenuous weeks together. He had nothing against the bushranger. He could not understand, either, why the sergeant should prevent him from walking over and nuzzling the man.

A plan was developing in the bushranger's mind concerning Blackie.

"How about letting us sit down, Potts?" he asked. "We've got a long time to wait for your fellow traps to get here."

"All right, Gibson, but don't try any funny business," warned the sergeant. Gibson and Wall sat down on the ground, their backs towards the fire. Potts watched them both closely, but could not do so all the time, hampered as he was by Blackie trying to make friends again with Gibson. He had to restrain the horse from approaching the outlaw. Definitely, the sergeant was in a dilemma.

Watching his chance, Gibson stealthily slid one hand behind his back, groping for a burning stick. His hand touched the hot ashes and though it burned him, he made no sign. The hand then grasped a burning stick by the hot end and quickly let it go. The next grope was luckier. His fingers closed round the unlighted end of a piece of wood.

With a sudden movement, he swung his arm in a circle and as he did so, the watchful Potts fired. The bullet struck the whirling hand, causing the bushranger to yell with agony. But he had completed his swing and the burning stick struck Blackie on the neck an clung there, the flame burning his mane.

The black stallion snorted and reared, jerking the reins from the sergeant's hand. Gibson, his hand wounded and burned, was unable to complete his plan to seize the horse, but Wall took advantage of the upset to make a dash. He felled Potts with a blow from his fist and flung himself at Blackie.

The brumby, still smarting under the indignity of having a lighted stick thrown at him, bucked and plunged as Wall tried to mount him and succeeded in hurling the bushranger to the ground. Sergeant Potts, whose gun had been knocked from his hand, saw the horse on hind legs towering over him, and quickly rolled out of the way. Wall, however, was not so lucky.

Blackie was very angry, and he showed it. The lighted stick had been dislodged from his mane, but the burned hair was enough to remind him of it. He pranced around for a moment on his hind legs, snorting madly, and then his iron-hard forefeet crashed down upon the prostrate bushranger.

Gibson, forgetting his burned and wounded hand, made a rush to seize Potts's pistol, but fell headlong over the body of his fallen mate, and crashed heavily. The sergeant got to his feet, dodged the still plunging brumby, and jumped clear. He scooped up his pistol and trained it on Gibson. His carbine was now lying on the grass, its strap having been broken when he fell down. With his heel he kicked it a few yards back, away from the bushranger. Wall was either unconscious or dead and could be counted out of the fight.

Flat on the ground, Gibson, looked up in terror as the dark form of the brumby blotted out the sun.

"Blackie, old boy," he said urgently. "It's me. Don't you know me, old chap?"

Blackie heard the voice and instead of dropping his hoofs straight down, slewed slightly away and came to rest within inches of the mans head. He then bent his own head and nuzzled the bushranger, who rolled over and stood up, panting with relief.

"It's all over now, Gibson," said Sergeant Potts. "Any more of your fancy tricks and I'll shoot you like the dog you are."

"You've still got to get me out of here, Potts," retorted the bushranger. Watched closely by the sergeant, he tugged from around his neck a large and dirty handkerchief and wound it round his wounded hand.

Potts was worried. He was in a fix and he knew it. He was thinking out a reply to the bushranger, when a loud shout arrested him.

"Jonah to the rescue!" roared the voice as that bright lad rode up on Ginger.

Jumping off, he unslung his rifle and trained it on Gibson.

"Two of us now, mate. How do you like that, huh?" he asked with a grin.

Gibson did not like it but did not trouble to say so.

"Who the dickens are you, and how did you get down here?" demanded the surprised sergeant.

"My name is Eric Jones, but call me Jonah. Eric is a sissy name. I'm a mate of George Sylvester," replied Jonah, and told Potts what had been transpiring since that officer had left the Spender store.

"I found my way here by asking an old goat I met along the road. A silly old coot he was, too. Said he had been robbed by bushrangers and that you were chasing them," he added.

"I'm certainly glad to see you, Jonah," said Potts. "Gibson. I'm going to handcuff you. Youngster, keep your rifle on him and if he makes a false move, shoot him. You'd be game to, I guess?"

"Game?" scoffed Jonah. "Listen, sergeant, I kill a bushie every morning before breakfast. I'll blow a hole clean through this bloke if he dares to even wink."

Thus assured, Potts told Gibson to mount his horse and when the outlaw did so, ordered him to put out his hands. Gibson obeyed and the sergeant deftly handcuffed him. He then took a length of rope from his saddlebag and tied the man's feet under the belly of the horse.

"Youngster," Potts then directed, "you mount your horse and take the reins of Gibson's horse. Lead him out of this gully on to the road. I'll ride behind and keep an eye on him."

"Righto, sergeant," said Jonah, slinging his rifle over his back and mounting Ginger. "What are you going to do about Wall's body? It makes the place look untidy, lying there."

"You're a hard-hearted little devil, Jonah," said Potts reprovingly. "We will send out and recover it later. Now, get moving."

The little cavalcade was half-way to the town when they met George Sylvester on Peter, accompanied by two troopers, Sinclair and McKenzie.

The sergeant told his fellow officers what had transpired and added, "This lad here did a first class job. I probably would have had a lot of trouble single-handed."

"No doubt about that, sergeant. You can always depend upon good old Jonah," said the owner of that distinguished name, quite without modesty, and Potts laughed.

"Blackie did a good job, too," put in George. "By the way, Jonah, where did you find old Ginger?"

"Straying near old Spender's store."

"You boys will probably share in the reward that has been offered by the Government for the arrest of Gibson and for ridding the country of that scoundrel Wall," said Sergeant Potts.

"That would be good-oh, but I'm quite repaid by having Blackie back," said George sincerely.

The sergeant instructed Trooper McKenzie to go to the scene of the fight, recover the body of the dead man Wall, and bring it, over the saddle of his horse, back to the police station. As McKenzie saluted and rode off on his dreary mission, Potts, Sinclair, George, Jonah and the sullen captive, Gibson, continued on their journey.

It was two very proud boys who rode into the township with the mounted troopers and their prisoner. George blushed a little at the cheers of the people who stopped to watch them go by, but Jonah took it all as his just right, even lifting his battered hat and bowing gracefully to several small girls who stood looking at the party in wide-eyed wonder.

Having lodged Gibson safely in the little lock-up with Trooper Sinclair on guard, Sergeant Potts announced himself as ready to go home with George and Jonah.

"I'd like to tell your father how you have behaved," he said and George expressed his gratitude. Not so Jonah.

"We can tell the yarn ourselves, George," said that lad in a whisper to his friend. "Old Potts might leave out all the best bits."

"Don't be so darned modest, Jonah," said George with a chuckle.

The sergeant secured another police horse while George mounted Blackie and Jonah transferred to Peter. George intended to lead Ginger.

"I want to ride Blackie to the house," he said. "It was my fault that he got stolen so I'd like to be the one to return him to Harry Hornsby," he explained.

"A bright notion, son," approved the sergeant. It was late afternoon when the trio pulled up outside the Sylvester residence. Telling George and Jonah to stay where they were, about a hundred yards from the homestead, the sergeant walked up the steps on to the verandah and knocked loudly. Old Sylvester himself answered the knock. He was accompanied by Harry Hornsby and the two men greeted the sergeant warmly.

"What can I do for you, Potts?" asked the squatter.

"It's about that boys of yours, and his friend Jonah," said the sergeant.

"What has George been up to now?" sighed his father wearily. "Seems to me I'll have to tan the hide off the lad one of these days."

"He's probably lost another horse, boss," put in Harry Hornsby, a trifle nastily.

"I'll tell you what he has been doing," said Potts. "He's been out shooting, riding horses all around the countryside and generally having a whale of a time. As for his friend Jonah, he bailed up a man with a rifle and threatened to shoot him, right under my very eyes!"

"Hey?" roared old Sylvester. "Say that again! Why, I'll kill the pair of them! Wait till I get my hands on them! Where the dickens are they?"

"Right there!" replied Potts, pointing.

"George!" bellowed his irate father. "Get down off that horse and come over here! I'm going to warm you, my lad, and no error! Why I'll..."

He broke off short.

"Dash my buttons!" he yelled. "That horse!"

"It's Blackie!" roared Hornsby, coming to life. "He's riding Blackie! Where did he get him?"

As Hornsby ran across the yard, Sergeant Potts quietly told Mr. Sylvester the complete story. The old squatter was silent for a long moment. He looked at George, who was now helping Hornsby to pat and fondle the appreciative Blackie, and he looked at Jonah, who was still sitting in the saddle on Peter.

Accompanied by the sergeant, he walked over to the little group and slammed George on the back.

"My son, I'm proud of you!" he said, his eyes beaming. "You are a great lad. A mighty fine boy."

"I'm not such a bad feller myself when you get to know me."

"You are certainly a number one hero, Jonah," smiled the squatter, and Jonah nodded his agreement.

Sergeant Potts stayed a few minutes chatting and then left. George turned to his father.

"What do you think of Blackie now, Dad?" he asked "You can't blame him for anything. If he was of help to Gibson as a bushranger, he also helped the police to get the two men, didn't he? Also, Dad, remember that Blackie was broken in on this station and was taught obedience. Gibson treated him well and Blackie obeyed him. It was what you, Harry Hornsby and Black Herbie taught him, you know."

Old Sylvester nodded his head slowly. Then he walked over to the big black stallion, looked him over for a moment in silence, and then stroked his nose gently. Blackie rubbed his head against the old man's coat.

"You'll do, Blackie," said the squatter. "You've made the grade. You are a true son of Margaret. She had good blood m her, and blood will tell."

"What about Bushranger?" said Hornsby slyly.

"Do you know what I think?" said old Sylvester seriously. "I wouldn't mind betting that Bushranger was a thoroughbred horse gone wild, too. He probably had good blood in his veins too."

Hornsby smiled behind his hand but said nothing.

"Blackie has the run of the station from now on," said the squatter. Picking up the reins, he led the black stallion into its old yard, where he personally unsaddled it and removed the bridle. Blackie threw up his head, whinnied and then dropped to the ground to roll luxuriously in the sand. Then, climbing to his feet, he advanced daintily to the squatter, his neck arched proudly. Rubbing his nose on the man shirt front, the brumby said as plainly as possible that he was glad to be home again and that old Sylvester was his friend.

Watching them affectionately, young George Sylvester turned to his friend Eric Jones.

"Gosh, but he's a marvellous horse!" he exclaimed.

"So am I," responded Jonah, absently.

THE END.